Tuscan Sunsets

A Scooter Journey Through Italy's Heartland

By
Well-Being Publishing

Copyright 2024 Well-Being Publishing. All rights reserved.

No part of this book may be reproduced in any form or by any electronic or mechanical means including information storage and retrieval systems, without permission in writing from the author. The only exception is by a reviewer, who may quote short excerpts in a review.

Although the author and publisher have made every effort to ensure that the information in this book was correct at press time, the author and publisher do not assume and hereby disclaim any liability to any party for any loss, damage, or disruption caused by errors or omissions, whether such errors or omissions result from negligence, accident, or any other cause.

This publication is designed to provide accurate and authoritative information with regard to the subject matter covered. It is sold with the understanding that the publisher is not engaged in rendering professional services. If legal advice or other expert assistance is required, the services of a competent professional should be sought.

The fact that an organization or website is referred to in this work as a citation and/or a potential source of further information does not mean that the author or the publisher endorses the information the organization or website may provide or recommendations it may make.

Please remember that Internet websites listed in this work may have changed or disappeared between when this work was written and when it is read.

Tuscan Sunsets

A Scooter Journey
Through Italy's Heartland

Contents

Contents 4
Introduction 1
Chapter 1: The Lure of Tuscany 4
Chapter 2: Preparing for Your Adventure 10
    Safety Tips and Gear 15
Chapter 3: Historic Cities and Hidden Gems 21
Chapter 4: Coastal Cruising and Seaside Escapes 30
Chapter 5: The Rolling Hills of Chianti 36
Chapter 6: The Gastronomic Journey 42
Chapter 7: Art and Soul of Tuscany 51
Chapter 8: Festivals and Seasonal Events 57
Chapter 9: Natural Wonders and Outdoor Activities 63
Chapter 10: Accommodations and Authentic Stays 70
Chapter 11: Extended Routes and Day Trips 76
Chapter 12: Tips and Tricks for the Savvy Scooterist ... 82
Sunset Reflections and the Road Ahead 89
Appendix A: Appendix 92

Introduction

Imagine the rolling hills of Tuscany, stretching far beyond the horizon, full of verdant vineyards, ancient olive groves, and roads that twist and wind like a dance through time. This is a landscape painted not just in earth and stone, but also in history, culture, and flavors that tantalize the senses. Your journey through this enchanting region is not just about seeing the sights; it's about experiencing Tuscany in a way that enriches your soul and invigorates your spirit.

Now, picture yourself exploring this idyllic countryside on a scooter. Riding a scooter in Tuscany offers a unique intimacy with the environment that can't be achieved through the window of a car or the aisles of a tour bus. You're not just passing through; you're a part of it all, feeling the cool breeze, smelling the fragrant blossoms, and hearing the distant hum of cicadas. On a scooter, every stretch of road becomes a personal experience, an opportunity for discovery and reflection.

For the curious traveler, Tuscany presents a myriad of opportunities to explore not only its landscapes but also its rich tapestry of culture and history. With a scooter as your trusted companion, you can venture off the beaten path, exploring hidden gems and quaint villages that might be overlooked otherwise. From the historic streets of Florence to the serene coastal vistas, Tuscany is a canvas waiting for your exploration.

A scooter trip doesn't just offer freedom; it grants unparalleled flexibility, permitting you to craft your own itinerary. Want to linger a while longer in a sun-dappled piazza, savoring gelato as you people-watch? Go ahead. Feel like taking a spontaneous detour to a local vineyard for a leisurely afternoon of wine tasting? The road is yours to claim. Every day is a new chapter in your Tuscan adventure, one where you hold the pen.

However, a journey of this sort isn't just about the places you visit. It's about embracing the Italian way of life, immersing yourself in the culture, and engaging with the people. Tuscan culture, renowned for its warmth and hospitality, welcomes those who are eager to learn, taste, and celebrate alongside its residents. By traveling on a scooter, you are participating in the rhythm and essence of life here, where community ties run deep and every meal is a celebration.

For tourists, scooter enthusiasts, and independent travelers alike, the prospect of exploring Tuscany on two wheels promises excitement and the creation of unforgettable memories. Whether you're a seasoned world traveler or a first-time explorer, the goal of this guide is to provide you with the tools, insights, and inspiration you need to embark on this adventure with confidence.

This guide is more than just a map of places to go or things to do. It's a companion on your journey, offering practical advice, cultural insights, and motivational encouragement to push beyond the commonplace and experience the extraordinary. You'll find tips on everything from safety and gear to navigating Tuscan terrain, ensuring that your trip is not only enjoyable but also well-prepared.

Dive into the chapters that follow, and you'll uncover Tuscany's historic cities rich with Renaissance art, scenic coastal roads where the sky meets the sea, and the endless charm of Chianti's rolling hills. We'll guide you through gastronomic tours that tantalize your palate, introduce you to local artisans who continue centuries-old traditions, and invite you to partake in festivals that light up the night with passion and heritage.

Whether you're planning a brief escape or an extended tour, the joys of Tuscany extend far beyond the ordinary travel experience. As you weave through landscapes that have inspired poets and painters, you'll be inspired too, discovering not just Italy's charms but also a deeper connection to the world around you.

So, as you prepare for your Tuscan adventure, remember that this journey is about embracing freedom, seeking out authentic experiences, and allowing the road to reveal the beauty of the world in a new light. Every mile you cover on that scooter will be a testament to the spirit of exploration and the joy of discovery. Welcome to Tuscany, where every turn has a story to tell, and each moment is an invitation to explore the extraordinary.

Chapter 1:
The Lure of Tuscany

In Tuscany, the rolling hills, golden fields, and sun-kissed vineyards whisper an invitation impossible to resist. As you navigate the picturesque roads on a scooter, every corner reveals a new delight; whether it's a quaint village frozen in time or sweeping landscapes that stretch as far as the eye can see. This journey promises more than just sightseeing; it offers an immersive dance with the region's vibrant culture and timeless beauty. The freedom of a scooter lets you weave through the land at your own pace, uncovering hidden idylls that beckon the soul of every adventure seeker. From the geniality of Tuscan hospitality to the fragrant aromas wafting from rustic trattorias, Tuscany charms all who wander its storied paths. Set against a backdrop where past and present blend seamlessly, this is where experiences turn into cherished memories, waiting to be embraced one twist of the throttle at a time.

Why Choose a Scooter for Your Journey? There's something undeniably captivating about exploring Tuscany on a scooter. It's not just about the wind in your hair or the liberating sensation of cruising along winding roads—although those are definitely bonuses. A scooter offers a unique way to connect intimately with the region, providing an experience that's both thrilling and deeply personal. Unlike a car, a scooter lets you feel the pulse of Tuscany, immersing you in its splendor, scents, and sounds as you glide over its rolling hills and through its charming towns.

Traveling by scooter allows you to venture beyond the traditional tourist paths. With this agile two-wheeler, narrow streets, secluded villages, and panoramic viewpoints are all within easy reach. If you've ever wanted to explore Tuscany like a local, a scooter is your ticket. Stop whenever the mood strikes—whether it's to admire a sprawling vineyard or to savor the charm of a local café that isn't on any guidebook's list. This freedom to explore at your own pace transforms your journey into a series of enchanting discoveries.

In many ways, a scooter embodies the essence of Tuscany itself. The region is renowned for its balance of the classic and the contemporary, and a scooter complements this duality perfectly. As you rev through the landscape, you'll find a seamless blend of history and modern life—from ancient architecture to vibrant city scenes. Riding a scooter means you're not just passing by these attractions but becoming a part of them, allowing you to feel the heartbeat of Tuscany firsthand.

It's not just the sites that make traveling by scooter so appealing. Consider the practicality: Tuscany's terrain, with its undulating roads and picturesque landscapes, seems tailor-made for scooter travel. You're afforded greater mobility, less worry about parking, and can effortlessly weave through traffic. Plus, scooters are typically more affordable to rent and maintain than cars, making them an accessible option for travelers on any budget. This practicality doesn't come at the cost of adventure; if anything, it enhances it by eliminating logistical concerns.

There's also an invigorating simplicity in choosing a scooter for your Tuscan journey. In a world dominated by complex travel plans and itineraries, sometimes stripping everything back to the basics allows you to enjoy a more pure experience. A scooter demands little—just you and the open road. This simplicity opens up ample opportunities to live in the moment and appreciate the little things that make travel rewarding. In Tuscany, these small moments could range from a chance meeting with a friendly local to the unexpected visual spectacle of a sunset over a vineyard.

For scooter enthusiasts and adventure seekers, Tuscany provides an exhilarating playground. It's an invitation tailored to those who thrive on spontaneity, who find joy in feeling the road underneath and the sun above, and who believe that the journey is just as important as the destination. The sense of adventure inherent in scooter travel mirrors Tuscany's own adventurous spirit—steeped in history yet always ready to surprise with something new.

Even for cultural explorers, a scooter isn't just a mode of transportation—it's a conduit to Tuscany's cultural richness. As you travel, you have the chance to truly absorb the local customs and traditions, engage with the diverse communities, and even participate in age-old festivities. This direct access to cultural happenings makes scooter travel in Tuscany an educational journey as well as a recreational one, broadening your understanding and appreciation of the region.

For independent travelers, the idea of charting their course through the Tuscan landscape is particularly appealing. Freedom and independence are hallmarks of scooter travel, allowing you to blaze your trail without the restrictions of public transport schedules or group tours. You are the architect of your adventure, choosing when to start, where to go, and how long to linger.

Scooter rental businesses in Tuscany have recognized this desire for independent exploration and have tailored their services to cater to a diverse clientele, offering everything from guided tours for those who prefer a bit more structure to simple rentals for the self-guided explorer. Their presence speaks volumes about the region's embrace of this unique travel method and the unforgettable experiences it facilitates.

The lure of Tuscany's scooter travel goes beyond mere convenience or adventure. It also touches on personal growth and inspiration. There's a certain confidence that comes from navigating the Tuscan roads, a boost to your adventurous spirit that stays long after the journey ends. Much like the indelible memories you'll create, this newfound self-assurance becomes a cherished souvenir of your travels.

In closing, choosing a scooter for your Tuscan journey means opening yourself up to a world of possibilities. It's about the visceral thrill of exploration, the simplicity of spontaneous travel, and the unparalleled connection to Tuscany's natural and cultural tapestry. Whether you're caught by the allure of its stunning vistas or its charming towns, a scooter enhances your experience, offering a truly immersive way to discover, celebrate, and remember Tuscany.

Understanding Tuscan Culture and Etiquette encompasses far more than just knowing a few Italian phrases or avoiding conversational faux pas. It's about embracing a way of life that cherishes simplicity, community, and a deep connection to the land. As you set out on your scooter to explore the rolling hills and historic cities, immersing yourself in Tuscan culture can significantly enrich your journey.

First and foremost, Tuscany values the art of slowing down. While the rest of the world seems to move at an ever-increasing pace, Tuscan culture urges you to take a step back and savor each moment. This is reflected in the region's unhurried routines and relaxed attitudes towards time. Meals are never rushed, and conversations might stretch on for hours. It's not uncommon for businesses to close for several hours in the afternoon, allowing people time to rest and recharge, a practice known as "riposo."

Another cornerstone of Tuscan life is the emphasis on family and community. Whether in a small village or a bustling city, the sense of belonging and support is palpable. Family gatherings are treasured events, often involving large meals where friends and neighbors might also be invited. As a visitor, being respectful and mindful of these tight-knit bonds is essential. Small gestures like a polite greeting or engaging in casual conversation over a coffee can go a long way in feeling connected to the community.

The Tuscan respect for nature, agriculture, and local produce is evident everywhere you look. It's a region rich in vineyards, olive groves, and fertile fields. The locals take immense pride in their products, which are celebrated not just for their taste but their connection to the land. Understanding this deep-seated love for locally sourced produce can enhance your appreciation for Tuscan cuisine. Participating in a wine tasting or visiting a farmer's market offers a glimpse into this cherished aspect of their culture.

Manners and politeness hold significant value. The use of "please" (per favore), "thank you" (grazie), and polite salutations like "buongiorno" (good day) or "buona sera" (good evening) is expected in daily interactions. It's equally important to respect personal space and quiet. Compared to the bustling streets of other Italian regions, Tuscan towns often have a serene and calm ambiance. You'll find that the locals appreciate discretion and gentle conversation tones, particularly in public settings.

The arts and humanities have long been intertwined with Tuscany's identity. The region's rich historical tapestry is not just restricted to museums or grand architecture. Tuscan art and craftsmanship are deeply rooted in everyday life. Strolling through its towns, you might encounter traditional artisans practicing age-old techniques. Engaging with local artists is not only an opportunity to learn but a chance to understand the cultural heritage that defines Tuscany.

Festivals and local events provide an authentic insight into Tuscan life. These events often revolve around historical commemoration, agricultural cycles, or religious rites. Participating, or even just observing, can offer deep insight into the cultural nuances of the region. The Palio in Siena, for instance, is more than a mere horse race; it's a centuries-old tradition filled with pageantry and emotion. Being part of such events requires sensitivity to local customs and practices.

Among the unwritten rules of Tuscan etiquette is the preference for understated elegance. The people of Tuscany tend to dress smartly yet modestly, embracing styles that reflect personal taste over fleeting trends. This approach extends to their homes and even personal interactions, which are often marked by genuine warmth and hospitality, rather than ostentation.

A pivotal aspect that might come as a surprise to newcomers is the deep respect for tradition coupled with openness to newcomers. Tuscans maintain a proud sense of identity while welcoming visitors with curiosity. It helps to approach conversations with respect for their customs and a genuine interest in learning. When discussing subjects such as history, art, or food, showing appreciation and admiration for their traditions can foster meaningful connections.

Exploring Tuscany by scooter offers the flexibility to discover hidden gems at your own pace. As you navigate its roads, remember that understanding and respecting local culture not only enhances your experience but adds depth and meaning to your travel story. The key to connecting with Tuscany isn't just in seeing its sights, it's in living through its rhythms, respecting its traditions, and engaging with its people. This harmonious blend of exploration and appreciation transforms a trip into an unforgettable journey.

Chapter 2:
Preparing for Your Adventure

As you prepare to explore Tuscany's rolling hills and charming byways on a scooter, envision a journey where spontaneity meets meticulous preparation. A seamless adventure in this picturesque region requires not just enthusiasm but a well-thought-out plan. It begins with understanding what essentials to pack for the varied Tuscan climate, ensuring you're comfortably outfitted no matter where the road leads. Equally important is choosing the perfect scooter, one that matches your style and suits the terrain, providing both reliability and thrill. Safety shouldn't be an afterthought; equipping yourself with the right gear guarantees peace of mind as you navigate winding roads. And don't forget navigational tools—be it digital maps or a classic compass—to guide you through Tuscany's captivating landscapes. Each decision sets the stage for a memorable and empowering journey, beckoning you to embrace the rustic elegance of Tuscany with confidence and an adventurous spirit.

What to Pack for a Scooter Trip Embarking on a scooter trip through the enchanting landscapes of Tuscany is undeniably exciting. But before you rev those engines, it's important to pack thoughtfully. The freedom of the open road, coupled with the charm of Tuscan towns, calls for smart packing that ensures comfort, safety, and convenience along your journey. From versatile clothing to essential gadgets, here's how to prepare for an unforgettable adventure on two wheels.

Well-Being Publishing

First and foremost, consider the apparel suitable for both riding and exploring. Layered clothing is a must, given Tuscany's varying temperatures—warm during the day and cooler in the evening. Pack breathable shirts, comfortable pants, and a lightweight jacket. Footwear should be both sturdy and comfortable; think along the lines of boots or sneakers that can withstand long walks in cobbled streets. Don't forget a packable raincoat or poncho, as Tuscany's weather can be unpredictable, with light showers appearing out of nowhere.

Your choice of bag is just as crucial as the clothes you bring. Opt for a compact backpack that is easy to wear while riding. It should be water-resistant to protect its contents from unexpected rain. If your travel plans include staying at different accommodations, a foldable daypack can be incredibly helpful for short excursions once your main bag is stowed safely away.

Safety gear, of course, is a priority. A good helmet isn't just a legal requirement; it's essential for your protection on those winding Italian roads. Depending on the season, you might also consider packing riding gloves and protective sunglasses. Gloves provide comfort over long rides, preventing blisters, while sunglasses protect your eyes from glare and dust.

For technology, a GPS device or smartphone with offline maps can be a lifesaver. Although the romantic idea of getting lost in Tuscany has its appeal, knowing how to find your way back is wise. Bring along a portable charger to ensure your devices remain powered—many a stunning Tuscan sunset has been missed due to dead batteries! If you're a photography enthusiast, a compact camera with extra memory cards is a great addition, allowing you to capture the vivid colors and textures of the Tuscan countryside without relying solely on your smartphone camera.

Then there are the small items that make a big impact. A reusable water bottle is a necessity—staying hydrated is vital as you zip through

Tuscan Sunsets: A Scooter Journey Through Italy's Heartland

vineyards and rustic villages. Sunglasses and a sun hat can offer essential protection from the sun, especially during the summer months. A travel-sized first aid kit with band-aids, antiseptic wipes, and pain relievers is always good to have on hand for minor injuries.

When it comes to sundry items, consider lightweight towels, especially if you plan a detour to one of the many famous thermal baths or a spontaneous swim along the coast. Also handy is a universal travel adapter to keep your electronics charged across different accommodations. If you're a lover of literature, a travel guidebook can serve as both a tactile map and a cultural companion as you navigate through the land known for its art and history.

The culinary landscape of Tuscany is a delight, so consider bringing a small picnic set. A foldable picnic blanket and reusable utensils make roadside lunches a festive affair under the Tuscan sun. Grab a map of local markets and keep a reusable tote bag handy for gathering fresh produce and specialties along the way. This way, you can create your own Tuscan delicacies wherever you choose to pause.

It's also important to pack with flexibility in mind. Remember that space is limited, so practice the art of rolling clothes to maximize space, and opt for travel-sized toiletries to lighten your load. Sharing some tips with your travel companions can also balance out the communal packing load, enabling each scooter to carry shared essentials.

Finally, pack an adventurous spirit. As you plan your luggage, remember that some of the best experiences in Tuscany come unexpectedly. Leave room for souvenirs and memories—those little things you can't anticipate but will treasure long after the trip concludes. With the right packing strategy, you're not just prepared for a journey; you're setting the stage for a series of unforgettable moments amidst Tuscany's serene landscapes and rich culture.

Selecting the Perfect Scooter can set the tone for your entire Tuscan adventure, so let's dive into what makes the ideal choice for navigating this picturesque region. Imagine winding through rolling hills, ancient olive groves, and vibrant vineyards on a scooter that feels just right in terms of comfort and capability. It's not just about picking any scooter but finding one that aligns with your travel preferences and the kind of experience you're seeking.

The first consideration is the type of roads you'll encounter during your travels. Tuscany is a land of varied terrains; the bustling avenues of Florence transition into narrow, cobblestone streets in smaller villages, sprawling vineyards, and undulating hills. For these diverse roads, scooters with good suspension systems, like a Vespa Primavera or a Piaggio Liberty, offer a smoother ride. These models provide an ideal balance between comfort and maneuverability, crucial for those unexpected sharp turns and occasional bumpy tracks.

Engine power is another vital factor. For short trips and city rides, a 50cc scooter might suffice. It's lightweight and easy to handle, perfect for darting through urban traffic and parking in tighter spots. However, if your itinerary includes longer jaunts through the countryside or the occasional incline, you might want to opt for a more robust engine, like a 125cc or 150cc. These models provide the additional power needed to tackle Tuscany's famous rolling hills and offer a more comfortable pace when traveling between cities.

Ergonomics can't be overlooked when selecting the perfect scooter. You'll be spending large portions of the day on your ride, and comfort should be a priority. Look for a scooter with a well-padded seat and sufficient legroom. Lombard Street in San Gimignano and the sweeping panoramas of Chianti are best enjoyed when you're not bothered by discomfort. Test how it feels to sit on the scooter, can your feet reach the ground easily when stopped, and check if your knees have room to move comfortably.

Tuscan Sunsets: A Scooter Journey Through Italy's Heartland

Storage space is crucial, especially if you're planning on carrying essentials like maps, water, sunscreen, or even a picnic. Many scooters offer under-seat storage, which can hold a small backpack or helmet. Some models have a rear luggage rack or top case that provides additional room. If you anticipate needing more storage, ensure this is a feature included or easily added to your chosen scooter.

Don't underestimate the role safety features play in your decision. Modern scooters often come with built-in safety mechanisms like anti-lock braking systems (ABS), which enhance control during hard stops—a necessity on those unexpected gravel patches or when a wild boar makes a surprise appearance. Make sure the scooter's headlights, indicators, and mirrors are in good condition too, ensuring excellent visibility during early mornings or late evenings.

You might also want to consider the rental company's reputation and customer support, especially in a country where you may not speak the local language fluently. Look for rental services with positive reviews, comprehensive insurance options, and round-the-clock assistance in case of emergencies. It's comforting to know you've got a reliable ally while exploring the winding roads of Tuscany.

Finally, take into account your familiarity and comfort with scooters. If you're a novice, it can be beneficial to rent a model similar to what you might have used before, as familiarity reduces risks of mishandling. For experienced riders, this trip could be the perfect opportunity to try out a new model.

Selecting the perfect scooter is akin to choosing a travel companion for your Tuscan adventure: it should complement your style, meet your travel needs, and enhance the journey. As you carve through the Tuscan landscape, you'll find that the right scooter not only enriches your experience but also becomes part of the story you take home. Embrace the journey, select wisely, and prepare for an unforgettable ride.

Safety Tips and Gear ...

As you gear up for a thrilling Tuscan adventure, ensuring your safety and comfort should be top of the list. Riding a scooter through the charming streets, undulating hills, and scenic coastlines offers unimaginable freedom and joy, but it also comes with its set of challenges. Understanding local road conditions, weather patterns, and how to handle your scooter responsibly can enhance your journey tenfold. Adventure enthusiasts will tell you that the right gear and safety precautions aren't just recommendations – they're necessities.

First and foremost, a well-fitted helmet is non-negotiable. Not only is it a crucial safety measure, but it's also the law in Italy. Investing in a high-quality helmet that snugly fits your head will help prevent any injury in the unfortunate event of an accident. Consider helmets with adequate ventilation and comfort linings, especially for those warm Tuscan days when you'll be spending hours on the road. Remember, safety doesn't compromise on style – helmets come in a variety of designs to suit your personality and taste.

Protective clothing is the next essential. While the idea of riding in a T-shirt and shorts might seem appealing, especially under the Italian sun, it's not always the safest option. Riding jackets and pants, made from sturdy materials like leather or reinforced textiles, can protect against scrapes and bruises. Choose lightweight and breathable fabrics that are comfortable for long rides, keeping you both safe and cool. Investing in gear with reflective strips can also enhance visibility during dawn, dusk, or unexpected downpours.

Gloves are another vital piece of gear often overlooked by new scooterists. They provide a better grip on the handlebars and protect your hands from blisters, wind chill, or potentially harsh sunlight. Opt for durable gloves that allow flexibility and tactility, ensuring you can maintain control of your scooter at all times. A pair of weather-resistant gloves can be a lifesaver if you find yourself caught in a sudden rainstorm, which isn't entirely uncommon in Tuscany's varied climate.

Footwear is equally crucial in completing your safety ensemble. While sandals might scream 'vacation,' they're not ideal for scooter travel. Durable boots or shoes should cover your ankles and provide solid footing, even on uneven terrain. Rubber soles are excellent for traction, helping you balance and maneuver better, especially when stopping and starting in busy town centers or rural pathways. Comfort is key; ensure your shoes are well-broken-in but robust enough to withstand a little wear and tear.

Beyond your personal gear, there are practical scooter accessories to consider. A windshield can protect you from bugs, dust, and wind, making your ride more enjoyable and safer. While Tuscany generally boasts lovely weather, having a rain cover or poncho stored in your scooter's compartment can be a wise move. A sudden shower can compromise visibility and make roads slick, so being prepared is essential to prevent mishaps.

Navigation plays an important role in maintaining safety. Before setting out each day, familiarize yourself with your route. Devices such as GPS can be incredibly helpful, but always have a backup plan. Paper maps or a mobile app like Google Maps can guide you through the charming, winding roads that technology might overlook. Always keep an eye on traffic signs and signals since they provide vital information on speed limits, turns, and potential hazards.

Stay tuned to local weather forecasts. Tuscany's weather varies significantly; while it might be sunny on the coastal fringes, the inland valleys could experience sudden fog or rain. Adjust your journey accordingly and set realistic expectations about what you can achieve in a day. If rain is forecasted, plan a later start or arrange indoor activities. Patience and being responsive to changing conditions can ensure your adventure is not just safe but also stress-free.

Lastly, be aware of your own limits, both physically and in terms of skill. If you're new to scooter riding, take some time to practice in a quiet area before hitting the busy streets. Get comfortable with starting, stopping, and maneuvering around obstacles. Don't hesitate to rent a smaller scooter if you're apprehensive; they're nimble and easier to handle, ideal for beginners or those more cautious about long rides.

Safety isn't just about preventing accidents; it's about ensuring your journey through Tuscany is memorable for all the right reasons. Embrace the essence of exploration with peace of mind, knowing you're well-prepared. With the right gear, attitude, and knowledge, you'll not only protect yourself but also enrich your adventure, opening the door to the countless cultural, historical, and natural wonders that Tuscany has to offer. So get ready, take these safety tips to heart, and enjoy the ride of a lifetime.

Navigational Tools for the Tuscan Terrain Navigating the picturesque yet intricate terrain of Tuscany is both a thrilling opportunity and a unique challenge. To truly experience the region's allure, from its endless vineyards and rolling hills to vibrant cities and tranquil coastal escapes, having the right navigational tools is essential. Whether you're riding through the bustling streets of Florence or venturing into the lesser-known countryside, these tools will enhance your journey, allowing you to explore with confidence and spontaneity.

In the age of technology, GPS devices and smartphone apps have revolutionized how independent travelers experience new destinations. Apps like Google Maps and Waze offer real-time updates and the flexibility to modify routes on the fly, ideal for those unexpected road closures or last-minute detours to hidden gems. Consider downloading offline maps, just in case you encounter those charming yet connectivity-challenged spots. Offline maps are particularly useful in areas where the cell signal might dwindle, allowing travelers to navigate without a hitch.

However, relying solely on technology in this ancient land can sometimes mean missing out on the richness of the traditional experience. A good old-fashioned paper map can act as your co-pilot, offering a tactile, visual understanding of the landscape. Maps provide perspective, showing how towns and landmarks connect in ways an app might not. Plus, there's no need to worry about battery life dwindling away when using a paper map. Seek out local tourist offices or bookshops for detailed maps that often offer more context about historical sites and cultural points of interest.

Language barriers might pose a challenge, but they also present an opportunity. Many modern tools offer language features to facilitate easier communication. Google Translate or similar apps could be your lifeline if you need to ask for directions or engage with locals who don't speak English. It's also worth learning a few essential Italian phrases; these can not only endear you to the local residents but also help you understand signage or directions more comprehensively.

For those who seek a more personalized adventure, consider hiring a local guide for a day or two. They're not just equipped with intricate knowledge of routes and trails less traveled, but can also introduce you to Tuscany's hidden treasures—places not marked on maps or known by apps. This kind of first-hand local insight can enrich your journey and allow for unexpected moments of delight, whether it's a secluded olive grove or an undiscovered artisanal shop.

Navigating Tuscan terrain on a scooter also requires attention to geographic and climatic conditions. That means tuning into local weather forecasts to determine the day's plans. Is it a perfect day for winding country roads, or is a storm looming that might make city streets easier to traverse? Road conditions can change with the seasons, as roads become more slippery when wet, or wildlife becomes more active at certain times of the year. Preparing for these scenarios can turn a potentially challenging situation into an anecdote-worthy adventure.

It's also essential to familiarize yourself with local traffic norms and signs. While scooters provide agility, it's crucial to adhere to speed limits and traffic regulations, especially on curvy and sometimes narrow Tuscan roads. Understanding basic Italian road signs—especially those indicating pedestrian zones or roundabouts—can help ensure a safe ride. Awareness of local driving etiquette is invaluable, whether you're navigating a bustling piazza or a tranquil rural avenue.

Another helpful resource is travel forums and communities, both online and offline. Websites like TripAdvisor and Lonely Planet host vibrant forums where travelers share recent experiences and tips specific to Tuscany. Engaging with these communities can offer insights into which routes are particularly scenic, where roadworks might be disrupting travel, and which small-town events might add an unexpected highlight to your trip.

As you prepare to set out into the Tuscan land of enchantment, it's vital to remember that the key to an enriching journey lies in adaptability and sense of exploration. While having tools available is beneficial, allowing yourself to occasionally wander off course can lead to the kind of discoveries that make travel memorable. Whether riding through the famed Chianti region or exploring coastal hideaways, the right blend of technology and tradition will anchor every twist and turn, inviting each traveler to craft a personal narrative woven through Tuscany's tapestry.

In the end, your soul will recall not just the routes you planned meticulously but those moments where Tuscany surprised you, challenging your expectations and expanding your horizons. With the right blend of navigational tools in hand, you're ready to embrace a side of Tuscany you can't find in travel brochures or maps—one that

Tuscan Sunsets: A Scooter Journey Through Italy's Heartland

captivates with its mix of spontaneity, tradition, and unyielding beauty.

Chapter 3:
Historic Cities and Hidden Gems

As you weave through the enchanting tapestry of Tuscany, each turn reveals a new chapter from the past. The historic cities and hidden gems offer a mesmerizing journey through time, ideal for those ready to explore beyond the well-worn paths. Imagine cruising into Florence, where the cradle of the Renaissance springs to life with every sculpture and fresco. Down the road, Siena stands as a medieval masterpiece, its towers and winding streets echoing tales of ancient rivalries and festal traditions. Yet, it's the lesser-known towns that whisper secrets only the adventurous hear, each brimming with untouched beauty and quaint charm. Embrace the freedom your scooter gives you, allowing spontaneous detours into sun-dappled alleys where artisans craft treasures passed down through generations. Whether it's a hidden terrace cafe offering panoramic vistas or a rustic trattoria serving regional delicacies, these small discoveries create memories that linger long after the journey's end. Tuscany invites you to write your own adventure, and the road less traveled becomes a mise en scène of dreams on your two-wheeled escape.

Florence: The Cradle of the Renaissance is much more than a magnificent city—it's truly a living, breathing testament to a time when art, science, and philosophy converged to reshape Western civilization. As you approach this iconic location on your scooter, you'll find that the journey is as exhilarating as the destination itself.

Tuscan Sunsets: A Scooter Journey Through Italy's Heartland

Picture this: the Italian sun kissing the rolling hills of Tuscany, with olive tree groves and vineyards painting an earthy palette, serving as a grand prelude to the splendor awaiting you in Florence.

Winding your way through the Tuscan countryside, you feel the anticipation building. This is a city where every street pulsates with stories; where cobblestones whisper the names of visionaries like Leonardo da Vinci and Michelangelo. The air seems different here—richer, as though imbued with the creative energy of those who dared to imagine beyond the constraints of their eras. The impact of their daring ideas and works still reverberates through the architecture and art dotting Florence's landscape.

Once you arrive in Florence, you immediately sense that it's a historian's dreamland and an explorer's playground. Navigating through its maze of narrow alleyways and charming piazzas by scooter offers a kind of freedom that traditional tours can't quite deliver. Stops at iconic sites like the embellished façade of the Florence Cathedral, also known as Il Duomo, or the geometrical brilliance of the Baptistery of St. John, these places are more than mere landmarks; they are narratives set in stone that have inspired continents and cultures.

A visit wouldn't be complete without wandering across the Ponte Vecchio. This medieval bridge is not just a crossing over the Arno River—it's a thriving market built on history. Forget the hustle and bustle for a moment as you take in the views along the riverbank and imagine the bustling life of Florence centuries ago. This historic cityscape invites you to lose yourself in its lanes, where every turn unravels another charm.

Beneath the sunlit ripples of the Arno, your scooter ride grants you the unique opportunity to stop wherever intrigue pulls you. You might find yourself drawn to the quieter squares like Piazza Santo Spirito, where artisans still craft leather and Florence's authentic atmosphere wafts on the breeze of everyday Tuscan life. Here's where the city's heart beats strongest, away from the guidebooks and itineraries.

But Florence is a city of layers. The Renaissance may be the facade that enchants, but delve deeper and discover hidden corridors of contemporary culture and creativity. Graffiti and modern art installations offer a stark yet complementary contrast to classical sculptures, creating a dialogue across centuries. Art isn't just housed in museums here—it spills out onto the streets, inviting every passerby to join in the ongoing conversation.

Of course, no dive into Florence would be complete without paying a visit to the Uffizi Gallery. Walking its hallowed halls, you're graced by works that command silence and awe. These masterpieces have survived revolutions and reconstructive epochs, standing not only as artistic triumphs but as resilient witnesses to the passage of time and its tumult. It's a humbling and invigorating experience to be in the presence of such history.

Your scooter serves as more than just a means of transport, it becomes a companion of convenience and camaraderie, allowing independent adventurers like yourself to pivot on a whim. Feel free to explore local cafes renowned for their cappuccinos and gelato stalls that promise a palette of flavors with textures so creamy they could only be Florentine.

Yet, it's not all about historic monuments and artistic grandeur. Florence's pulse is found in its people—in their affection for insertions of community festivals. Almost every day, there's a celebration of some kind, whether it's honoring a saint, igniting long-held family traditions, or rejoicing in the joys of contemporary life. These gatherings shine a light on Florence's values, emphasizing community, unity, and vibrancy. As a visitor, you're welcomed not just to observe but to join in.

Tuscan Sunsets: A Scooter Journey Through Italy's Heartland

One can't overlook Florence's culinary scene—each meal a celebration infused with ages-old recipes. Delicate plates of pappardelle al cinghiale tell tales of regional tastes, while glasses of Florentine wines sort memories into comfortable corners of your mind. Winding your day down with a feast allows you to reflect on your experiences as the sun sets over a city that's timeless, filling the sky with hues that seem to echo the mesmerizing artistry beneath.

As the city lights begin to illuminate Florence's charming streets, there's a new dimension to behold. Discover hidden terraces where live music sets the tone for enchanting evenings intertwined with local stories. It's here, under the gentle glow of lamplight, that the people of Florence both honor their past and embrace their future, securing the city's place in history as a guiding star of creativity and resilience.

Florence is more than an open-air museum; it's a destination of transformation. It inspires those who open their hearts and minds, offering the essence of the Renaissance—a movement that was never just about the revival of art and culture but about the awakening of human potential and creativity. Leave Florence not merely having seen the sights but inspired, equipped with your own dawn of discovery and maybe even a little of its enchanted spirit to guide your wandering heart on journeys yet to come.

Siena: A Medieval Masterpiece nestled snugly amid Tuscany's rolling hills, Siena stands as a splendid testament to medieval craftsmanship and heritage. As you crest a hill on your scooter, the city unravels like a tapestry, with its world-renowned fan-shaped Piazza del Campo at the heart. The rust-red bricks of the city walls and the soaring Torre del Mangia signal a journey back in time, where history is palpably etched into every street and alleyway. Siena isn't just a place to visit; it's a way to immerse yourself in a medieval world that remains vividly alive.

The city's labyrinthine streets are a scooter enthusiast's dream. Winding through the narrow alleys of Siena offers a sense of adventure and discovery. Imagine weaving through paths that curve and turn, where every corner reveals an architectural marvel or a quaint bakery emitting tantalizing aromas of fresh pastries. Here, the roads guide you on a journey through time, leading you to taste a slice of Tuscan life from centuries past.

History buffs will find Siena to be an absolute marvel. The city has lovingly preserved its Gothic architecture, a feat that makes it a UNESCO World Heritage Site. The stunning Cathedral of Santa Maria Assunta is an artistic treasure trove, showcasing works by Donatello, Michelangelo, and Bernini. Walking inside is like stepping into an elaborate art gallery that tells stories of devotion and artistry through its intricate mosaics and vibrant frescoes.

The Palio di Siena is an exhilarating spectacle that takes place twice a year, in July and August. This historic horse race pits the city's various districts or contrade against one another in a spirited contest of skill and rivalry. If you time your visit right, watching the Palio from your scooter is an experience you won't forget—a burst of color, sound, and tradition compressed into a few thrilling minutes.

But Siena is not just about its past; it's a living city, brimming with culture and activities. Dotted with charming trattorias and enotecas, it offers a gastronomic journey that indulges the palate with traditional Siena dishes, like the savory ribollita or the irresistible panforte. Each meal is not merely tasting food, but savoring the unique essence of the Sienese lifestyle.

Visiting Siena gives you a chance to engage with the locals, who are fiercely proud of their city and its rich traditions. Engaging with them, even in a casual chat over a cappuccino, can provide insights into a life steeped in history and pride. Siena teaches its visitors that sometimes the heart of a city isn't just in its landmarks, but in its people.

Tuscan Sunsets: A Scooter Journey Through Italy's Heartland

The adventure doesn't end when you leave the city limits. The surrounding countryside offers undulating landscapes ripe for exploration on a scooter. The Val d'Orcia, with its captivating vistas of cypress-lined roads and vast vineyards, invites you to take unhurried rides and inhale the beauty of nature interwoven with centuries of history. Each ride from Siena can be a meditation, a chance to reflect on the interlocking stories of man and earth.

For those in search of artistic inspiration, Siena's influence extends beyond its formal confines. Visits to local workshops and galleries reveal how the city's history permeates into contemporary art. Watch artisans craft pottery in centuries-old traditions, and see how the past is reinvented in each brushstroke or pottery mold. Siena allows for a dialogue between the past and the present that can ignite new ideas within an artist's mind.

Siena's status as a medieval masterpiece is not confined to its physical structure but resonates in its festivals, lifestyle, and vibrancy. The city presents a grand narrative that embraces both timeworn continuity and the contemporary spirit. Whether you're drawn to Siena for its cultural intrigue, the thrill of exploration on scooters, or simply the allure of experiencing a place where time seems to stand still, the city opens itself to be discovered, savored, and remembered.

In the broader landscape of Tuscany, Siena truly is a jewel in the crown, inviting you to explore its charms with an open heart and a sense of adventure. There's something freeing about breezing through its streets on a scooter, the wind in your hair, the promise of discovery awaiting at each turn, and the knowledge that you are treading paths shared by generations before you. It's not just a visit; it's a journey through time, wrapped in the beauty and wonder of a living medieval masterpiece.

Lesser-Known Towns Worth a Visit weave a tapestry of experiences that paint Tuscany in earthy, vibrant tones away from the usual haunts. These towns, nestled between iconic destinations, are threads in the rich fabric of history, culture, and natural beauty that define the region. For those looking to straddle adventure with curiosity and a sense of wonder, these charming locales offer experiences that are both time-honored and unexpected.

Cetona, with its medieval soul, lies serenely at the foot of its namesake mountain. This quaint town lets you wander through narrow streets that hold whispers of a storied past. The main square, Piazza Garibaldi, is a hub of local life where you can enjoy a glass of local wine while soaking in views of Mount Cetona. The surrounding lush countryside offers trails perfect for the outdoor enthusiast, leading you through olive groves and vineyards—a scooter ride here is a journey into tranquility.

Another gem is San Miniato, perched on a hill midway between Pisa and Florence. Its strategic location historically made it a point of contention and prosperity. Today, San Miniato is renowned for its white truffles, celebrated with a festival each November. As your scooter winds through its countryside, you'll pass by fields and forests, vibrant in the autumn months. The town itself offers a slew of architectural delights, from the Torre di Federico II to the Cathedral of Santa Maria Assunta – testaments to its rich past.

The village of Montecarlo unfolds as an enchanting destination for wine and history enthusiasts alike. Known for producing some of Tuscany's finest whites, Montecarlo invites you to its storied cellars, where wine-tasting becomes an act of communion with the land. The fortress, Fortezza di Montecarlo, offers panoramic views that tell stories of a bygone era when the town shielded Lucchese territory. Stroll through its charming streets, and discover artisan shops offering local wares that speak of time-honed traditions.

Moving slightly off the tourist path, Suvereto is a pleasure waiting to be explored. Located near the Etruscan Coast, it blends the charm of hilltop settings with the allure of history. The town is a canvas of ancient stone buildings and vibrant life, where scooters provide a modern pulse against timeless backdrops. Suvereto's Romanesque churches and medieval fortifications belie a rich lineage that beckons explorers. Make your way to the Rocca Aldobrandesca and experience its breathtaking vantage points—rewarding efforts for those willing to journey beyond the immediate horizon.

Radicofani serves as another captivating stop, set on a basalt cliff in the southernmost part of Tuscany. Its striking Rocca fortress commands the skyline, standing as a sentinel over the Val d'Orcia landscape. Scooter your way through its steep streets, and let the stories of Ghino di Tacco, the legendary Robin Hood-like figure, enchant your journey. The views from the fortress alone, stretching across a tapestry of untouched natural beauty and historical intrigue, make this a noteworthy detour.

Bemused by the quieter pull of nature? Explore the rolling fields and hidden alleys of Giglio, a diminutive island with a heart louder than its size, located off the Tuscan coast. It offers an intimate escape where rustic paths lead to hidden coves and sparkling waters. Riding a scooter here feels like gliding over the Mediterranean: an experience that's as refreshing as it is invigorating. The island's crystalline beaches and charming harbor town of Giglio Porto whisper stories of a seafaring past, blending land and sea in a harmony unique to Tuscan islands.

Lastly, Castiglione di Garfagnana perches atop the lush hills of the Garfagnana area. Its walls enfold a community and history that's palpable in its very stones. Explore the Rocca Ariostesca, the castle named after poet Ludovico Ariosto, and wander the scenic routes around the town. The Apuan Alps backdrop serves as a stunning canvas where each turn reveals another breathtaking view. Here, the air is fresh, the pace is slow, and the opportunities for exploration by scooter are boundless.

These lesser-known towns embody the spirit of discovery—the romance of the road and the quiet allure of hidden treasures. With each town offering its unique blend of history, culture, and natural beauty, the allure of Tuscany unfurls anew with every scooter journey taken. Whether you're weaving through vineyards or pausing atop ancient fortresses, every visit to these quieter corners becomes a part of your own Tuscan narrative, encouraging independent exploration and fostering a personal connection to this timeless land.

Chapter 4: Coastal Cruising and Seaside Escapes

Imagine gliding along the sun-drenched roads of the Tuscan coast, a gentle breeze brushing against you as you discover the region where azure waves kiss golden shores. Here, the journey is as mesmerizing as the destinations themselves. The coastline offers a unique blend of vibrant coastal towns and secluded beaches, each sharing the rhythm of the Mediterranean. Cruising the Etruscan Coast on a scooter lets travelers immerse themselves in the area's rich history while enjoying breathtaking vistas at every turn. The salty air invigorates as you navigate winding paths, leading to quiet coves and bustling harbors, each revealing a story waiting to be discovered. Island hopping becomes an adventure, with ferries whisking you off to explore nearby islands, where each stop promises new experiences grounded in the timeless beauty of the Italian seascape. Indulging in this chapter of Tuscany by scooter transforms travel into an unforgettable escape—an odyssey set against the backdrop of a sunlit sky and the endless possibilities of the sea.

The Etruscan Coast: Beaches and Beyond offers a refreshing escape from the hustle and bustle of Tuscany's historic cities. Imagine the gentle swoosh of the sea breeze as you cruise along the coast, with the shimmering Tyrrhenian Sea on one side and lush, rolling hills on the other. This area, also known locally as "Costa degli Etruschi," is much more than just its stunning shoreline. It's a rich tapestry of archaeological marvels, picturesque vineyards, and quaint little towns brimming with history and character.

As you embark on this scooter journey, you'll quickly realize that the Etruscan Coast is famed not only for its beaches but also for its profound historical significance. The ancient Etruscans, who predate Roman civilization, once thrived here, leaving behind a cultural and architectural legacy that shapes the region today. From grand necropolises to small archaeological sites, history buffs and casual tourists alike will find these relics fascinating.

Peer into the past at Populonia, one of the few coastal Etruscan cities. Here, you can wander through the well-preserved ruins that huddle against the sparkling sea, offering a smartphone-less glimpse into a world long forgotten. As you explore, the rustle of olive trees and the warmth of terracotta structures whisper stories of ancient rituals and bustling marketplaces. The Museo Etrusco in nearby Piombino further enriches your journey with artifacts that piece together untold tales of Etruscan life.

Of course, no coastal exploration is complete without indulging in the beaches. The Etruscan Coast boasts an astounding variety, from wide sandy stretches perfect for sunbathing to hidden coves where serenity reigns. One moment you're lounging on the golden sands of Rosignano Solvay — its strikingly turquoise waters inviting you for a swim — and the next, you're navigating the rugged pathways to Baratti's pebbled beach, tucked within a bay framed by pine forests and old-world charm.

Baratti holds another draw. It's a favored spot for sailing and windsurfing, where sea enthusiasts slice through azure waves, the wind caressing their faces. This picturesque bay is not only about aquatic adventures; it's also bordered by trails perfect for an afternoon hike or a leisurely walk, providing vistas so stunning they seem painted by an artist's brush.

A journey along the Etruscan Coast certainly wouldn't be complete without savoring the regional cuisine. Seafood lovers will be in paradise, with fresh catches like carpaccio di pesce spada (swordfish carpaccio) or the renowned cacciucco, a hearty seafood stew that exudes local robustness with every bite. Dining in small trattorias or seaside cafes, you'll encounter menus that change with the tides, each dish a testament to the area's rich maritime heritage.

Then there are the wine routes. The coast is home to some of Italy's most revered vineyards, tucked away in the charming hillsides. Consider visiting Bolgheri, a picturesque village that's synonymous with prestigious wines. Cruise your scooter along cypress-lined roads leading to esteemed wineries such as Ornellaia and Tenuta San Guido, where the world-famous Sassicaia is crafted. Here, the art of winemaking is as much about passion and tradition as it is about the exquisite taste notes that linger on your palate.

For those with an adventurous spirit, venturing inland from the coast offers more surprises. Small towns like Castagneto Carducci beckon with cobbled streets and rustic architecture, each turn revealing hidden vistas that beg to be captured on camera or in memory. Named after the famed poet Giosuè Carducci, this town provides a snapshot of Tuscany's quintessential charm and hospitality.

The Etruscan Coast isn't just a destination; it's a symphony of experiences that resonates long after the journey ends. Whether you're drawn to the allure of its beaches, the whispers of its ancient past, or the rich flavors of its vineyards, this journey on two wheels promises to be anything but ordinary. The freedom of a scooter allows you to weave seamlessly between moments of reflective tranquility and thrilling adventures. With every mile traveled, you're immersed deeper into the heart of Tuscany, discovering its secrets and creating your own stories along the way.

Island Hopping on Two Wheels offers a unique and exhilarating way to explore Tuscany's coastal islands, where turquoise waters embrace the lush landscapes and history whispers through the coastal breeze. Picture this: the salty spray kissing your cheeks as you zip along the coastlines, past cliffs that dramatically plunge into the azure sea. Scooters provide not just a means of transport, but a ticket to freedom and exploration, unlocking areas of Tuscany many don't venture to when confined by traditional travel.

In this section, we'll journey to some of Tuscany's enchanting islands, each accessible by ferry or bridge. Your scootering adventure can start from Piombino, where ferries await to whisk you over to these island paradises. Once you're on two wheels, the islands unfold in spectacular fashion, offering both leisurely cruises and adrenaline-packed rides across diverse terrains.

First on our list is the Island of Elba, a gem known for its historical significance and natural beauty. Napoleon Bonaparte himself was exiled here, and as you traverse the island, you'll find nods to his legacy in towns like Portoferraio. Rider-friendly roads snake through vineyards and golden beaches. Each turn seems to offer a view more breathtaking than the last, urging even the most focused adventurer to pause and soak it all in. The island's varied topography, from craggy cliffs to serene coves, promises plenty of exploration right from your scooter's seat.

Venture further to Giglio Island, where the vibrant green hills contrast against the twinkling blues of the Tyrrhenian Sea. Here, the rustic charm of the villas and the quaint squares of Giglio Porto greet you warmly. The roads, though narrow, are well-maintained, making the ride seamless and meditative. Experience the peace as early mornings unveil misty panoramas and the sun dapples through olive groves, transforming daily rides into magical journeys.

For those seeking a quieter escape, the Island of Capraia offers an environment so untouched, you'll feel far removed from the mainland's bustle. Capraia boasts a singular paved road perfect for scooters — it winds from the ferry port through the town and into the island's volcanic heart. This is an island for savoring silence, where time slows, and the whispers of the island's past are more audible. Riding here isn't just about reaching a destination; it's about the intimate interaction with nature along the way.

These islands each have their own rhythm, flavors, and stories; and on two wheels, you become part of this living tapestry. Beyond the thrill of scootering, there's much to immerse yourself in. Elba's rich mineral history invites you to explore its mines, while Giglio's vineyards roll out the exquisite vintages, drawing you to intimate tastings that are a feast for the senses. Capraia's secluded bays call for a swim after a ride through its rugged hills, where the journey leads directly into azure waves.

Interspersed between rides, the culinary experiences delight. Elba tempts with schiaccia briaca, a dessert whose significance dates back to the 16th century. On Giglio, enjoy prosciutto carved directly in front of you, or perhaps sample fresh seafood at a harborside trattoria while your scooter rests nearby. Capraia's sparse settlements offer less restaurant variety, but the few present serve dishes as rich in flavor as they are fresh from the sea.

As you explore these islands by scooter, keep in mind the importance of sustainable travel. Small adjustments, like using public ferries and supporting local businesses, have a big impact. Additionally, staying in eco-friendly accommodations and respecting the rich ecosystems by following local guidelines ensures these magical destinations remain pristine for future adventurers.

The fusion of freedom, adventure, and cultural immersion that comes from island hopping on two wheels in Tuscany is unmatched, providing endless opportunities for unexpected discoveries. You'll find this style of travel awakens the explorer within, inspiring a connection deeper than just from one sight to another. It's about becoming part of the fabric of each island, weaving your own story through the roads you travel.

In the end, these scooter adventures aren't just about the places you visit but the transformative journey itself. Embrace the ride, and let Tuscany's islands reveal themselves to you as only they can from the vantage point of two wheels.

Chapter 5:
The Rolling Hills of Chianti

Embrace the charm of Chianti's rolling hills as they unfurl like an artist's masterpiece, brushing the horizon with lush vineyards and silvery olive groves. This region beckons travelers with roads that wind through valleys and offer soul-stirring views, perfect for a scooter adventure. As you navigate these scenic routes, the air is rich with the fragrance of cypress trees and the promise of discovery at every turn. Chianti isn't just a landscape; it's a cultural tapestry interwoven with the art of winemaking and a rhythm of life that invites exploration. From family-run vineyards that welcome you like kin to secluded paths whispering of stories untold, these hills are more than just a backdrop—they're an invitation to experience Tuscany's heart with an unparalleled intimacy. Go ahead, let the spirit of adventure guide you as the scooter becomes your trusted companion in tasting the essence of Chianti, glass by glass, mile by mile.

Vineyards, Olive Groves, and Scenic Routes are the heart and soul of Chianti, offering an intoxicating blend of natural beauty and cultural richness. Imagine cruising on a scooter along winding roads that snake through the countryside, with verdant hills rolling out as far as the eye can see. The experience is nothing short of euphoric. It's not just about the destination; it's the journey itself that captivates. The air is crisp and scented with an earthy mix of fertile soil and ripening grapes, while the sun bathes the landscape in a golden hue.

Chianti, renowned worldwide for its iconic wines, is a tapestry of vineyards that stretch in perfect lines across the hills. These vineyards are a testament to centuries-old traditions that unite with the land in harmony. While exploring, you might witness the grape harvest, known as the "vendemmia," a time of celebration and hard work that fills the region with vibrant energy. The local vignerons (winemakers), often proud to share their family stories, play a vital role in preserving this heritage.

As you ride through this enchanting land, olive groves present themselves as another integral part of the Chianti landscape. Like the vineyards, olive trees have deep roots here, producing some of the finest olive oils in the world. The dance of silvery-green leaves under a gentle breeze creates a mesmerizing effect, and when in season, the scent of olives being pressed is both earthy and enticing. It's easy to stop by a family-run olive mill and learn the intricacies of creating liquid gold, an experience that enriches your appreciation of simple, authentic flavors.

On two wheels, you become a part of the scenery, able to stop at a moment's notice to capture the picturesque views that Chianti so generously provides. There's no rush—each small village you pass beckons with charm and invites you to linger. Stone houses with terracotta roofs, geranium-filled window boxes, and narrow, cobblestone streets make a perfect backdrop for your tuscan exploration. These villages, each with its own personality, offer a glimpse into a way of life that cherishes tradition and simplicity.

For adventurers seeking more than just visual splendor, the routes through Chianti offer a dynamic range of activities. Off the beaten path, trails invite hikers and cyclists to discover secluded spots where nature reigns supreme. However, for the scooterist eager for discovery, it's the allure of endless roads that twist and turn through sun-drenched landscapes that captivate the spirit. Embrace the exhilaration of freedom as you embark on less-traveled roads that reveal stunning vistas around every bend.

The routes aren't just about grandeur; they carry historical significance too. Along the way, you'll encounter signs of ancient Etruscan settlements and medieval strongholds, whispering tales of yore. Castles perched on hilltops, once vital outposts, now serve as picturesque reminders of the region's storied past. They stand tall and proud, each with its own narrative that's worth exploring.

In Chianti, the road does more than lead the way; it unveils a tapestry rich with life. It encourages the kind of mindfulness often forgotten in the hustle and bustle of modern life. Scootering through this landscape affords travelers the opportunity to connect deeply with their surroundings and perhaps even with themselves. It's therapeutic in its simplicity, offering moments of introspection as you glide through this artful blend of humanity and nature.

Such journeys spark an appreciation not only for the land but also for the passionate people who call Chianti home. Whether it's a local artisan telling stories of traditional craftsmanship over espresso or a farmer eagerly showcasing their produce at a roadside stand, the warmth of the Chianti community enriches every mile traveled. Each encounter emphasizes the unique identity of this land, where community and connection are cherished.

To fully embrace the Chianti experience, step off your scooter at a local taverna to enjoy authentic Tuscan cuisine. Discover the rustic flavors that define regional eating, from freshly baked bread dipped in local olive oil to hearty bowls of ribollita. Pair your meal with a glass of Chianti Classico, and reflect on the day's journey. It's these moments of culinary indulgence that complete the rich tapestry of your travel narrative, leaving you with memories that linger long after you've returned home.

Finally, remember the endless sky above and the rolling hills below. Under the Tuscan sun, everything seems possible. The vineyards, the olive groves, and the scenic routes—all serve to remind you that exploration can be as boundless as the landscape itself. As you continue onward, carry with you the spirit of freedom, the allure of discovery, and the tranquil beauty of the Chianti countryside. The roads are waiting, and so are the adventures that lie just beyond the horizon.

Wine Tasting by Scooter Picture the sun-dappled hills of Chianti unfolding before you as you rev the engine of your trusty scooter. The rolling vistas beckon you to explore their treasures, and among these, the vineyards stand as a testament to the region's opulent relationship with wine. With the wind in your hair and the promise of discovery, wine tasting by scooter offers a unique interplay of freedom and indulgence that few modes of travel can rival.

Chianti, celebrated for its alluring landscapes and exceptional wines, presents a perfect backdrop for this adventure. As you weave through the cypress-lined roads, each twist and turn reveals a new vista—vineyards stretching into the horizon, their geometric lines punctuated by the charming silhouette of a rustic farmhouse. A ride through these paths is not just a journey from point A to point B; it's an immersive experience in the lush tapestry of Tuscany's viticultural heritage. Imagine pulling over at a family-owned winery where the owners greet you with stories as rich and complex as the Chianti Classico they're pouring.

The incentive to embark on a scooter-led wine tour is manifold. There's the sheer joy of unhindered travel—the kind that lets you meander at your own pace, stop spontaneously at a lookout point, and savor the moments that mainstream tours might whisk by. Your scooter becomes your passport to hidden cellars and out-of-the-way tastings. It's about embracing the journey as much as the destination and relishing the tactile experience of traveling roads less traveled.

Look to pair your rides with visits to some of the renowned vineyards that dot this region. These estates are often blessed with both age and acclaim, having honed their craft over generations. Consider the likes of Castello di Brolio, a majestic estate known not just for its wine but also its rich history dating back to the noble Ricasoli family. A visit here invites you to explore the castle's gardens, where centuries-old tales seem to whisper along with the breeze.

While the larger, more famous wineries have their enchantments, don't overlook the smaller, boutique vineyards. These lesser-known gems offer a more intimate glimpse into winemaking. Their vintages might not have the same global recognition, but they offer a taste of innovation and individuality fostered by family tradition. It's here that you might find a vintner eager to share the nuances of each sip, guiding you through flavors that are as varied as the expressions on Chianti's vibrant landscape.

Every visit introduces you to a different facet of the wine world, from robust Sangiovese to elegant Vin Santo, inviting you to broaden your palate with tastings paired with local delicacies. The quality and depth of flavor found in Tuscan wines, coupled with the genuine hospitality of the vineyard owners, ensure that every stop on your itinerary feels like a personal discovery.

A satisfying aspect of touring by scooter lies in the versatility and flexibility it offers. You'll weave through the countryside, deciding on a whim to explore small towns that flank your route. Picture a spur-of-the-moment detour to Greve in Chianti, with its charming piazza lined with artisanal shops and cafes perfect for a relaxed espresso break. Or maybe you'll venture towards Panzano, drawn by the prospect of a leisurely lunch featuring regional fare at a 'trattoria' with a reputation among locals.

However, amid this freedom, safety must not take a backseat. Make sure to plan your route in advance, allowing for scheduled stops and ensuring you're well aware of speed limits and local traffic laws. Part of the charm of exploring Chianti by scooter is the slower, more immersive pace, allowing for breaks where you can take in the panoramic views safely and without haste. Hydration and sun protection are key, especially in the sunlit months when the Tuscan sun shines brightest. Remember that moderation is essential; savoring wine is a sensory experience meant to be enjoyed responsibly.

Embarking on a scooter wine tour is more than adding another tick to a traveler's checklist; it's about engaging all your senses. Imagine the blend of scents—the earthy aroma of the vineyard, the warm, rural air blending with the perfume of ripe grapes ready for harvest. It's these sensory intricacies that make the journey unforgettable. As you return your scooter to Chianti's rolling hills at the end of a satisfying day, bask in the richness of Tuscany's offerings and the new stories you've gathered around each bend. This adventure invites you to dive deeper into the tapestry of Tuscany, to savor its wine, and to move through its landscapes with a sense of wonder and respect.

Chapter 6:
The Gastronomic Journey

Embarking on Tuscany's gastronomic journey offers more than just a feast for the palate; it's an exploration into the heart and soul of a region renowned for its culinary heritage. Savory scents waft from trattorias where generations-old recipes tell tales of family and tradition. Picture gliding through rolling hills dotted with olive groves and vineyards, each stop offering a different taste of Tuscany's culinary treasures. At bustling local markets, vibrant colors and fresh aromas beckon visitors, offering a blend of rustic street food and artisan delights—perfect morsels to enjoy on a sun-dappled piazza with a view of ancient architecture. Cooking classes invite you to go beyond the superficial tastes, encouraging a hands-on discovery of preparing simple yet profound dishes that echo Tuscany's rich history. This gastronomic journey isn't just about indulging in food, but about embracing the essence of Tuscan life, fostering connections over shared meals, and carrying back with you not just flavors, but stories immortalized in every delectable bite.

Savoring Tuscan Cuisine delves into a culinary adventure that is nothing short of transformative for any traveler traversing this enchanting region. Picture yourself winding through the sun-dappled hills of Tuscany on a scooter, your senses already enticed by the promise of impeccable Italian flavors. Tuscan cuisine is not just about eating; it's a celebration of the land, its produce, and a deep-seated culture that takes food as seriously as art.

In Tuscany, meals are a ritual that transcends mere sustenance. It's a communal affair, often stretching into the late hours as friends and family gather around tables laden with simple yet exquisite dishes. Bread is a staple, but not just any bread—the crusty, saltless pane Toscano is a testament to the region's agrarian roots and resourcefulness. Served alongside a fiery bruschetta drizzled with golden olive oil, you're apt to find yourself appreciating the simplicity and purity of fresh, local ingredients.

The heart of Tuscan fare lies in its unwavering respect for high-quality, seasonal ingredients. The countryside abounds with myriad flavors, from the hearty ribollita, a warming stew crafted from carefully selected vegetables and rustic bread, to the revered bistecca alla fiorentina. This renowned T-bone steak, hailing from Florence, is cooked with precision and simplicity, allowing the quality of the Chianina cattle beef to shine, seasoned with little more than salt, pepper, and perhaps a sprig of fresh rosemary.

Venture into the rolling landscapes where vineyards and olive groves dot the scenery, and you'll discover an essential tenet of Tuscan cuisine—its robust wines and oils. Chianti, with its ruby-red allure, is more than a beverage; it's a staple at every meal, harmonizing beautifully with rich flavors and enhancing the dining experience. Don't miss sampling Tuscany's olive oils, which range from smooth to peppery; they're often poured generously over soup, bread, or roasted vegetables, adding a depth of flavor that's authentically Tuscan.

Then there's the cheese. From the sharp, aged pecorino of Pienza to the fresh ricotta dolloped onto pasta or nestled within fluffy gnocchi, cheese is an integral part of many dishes. It's the creamy pairing for fruits like ripe figs or luscious pears and pairs exquisitely with a glass of Vernaccia di San Gimignano, a white wine known for its crisp, mineral bite.

Tuscan Sunsets: A Scooter Journey Through Italy's Heartland

Dining in Tuscany isn't all about the food that's served; it's about the experience, the ambiance, the melding of flavors, and the stories each dish tells. Wander into local trattorias where Nonna may rule the kitchen, stirring pots of rich ragù or tossing delicate pici pasta. Or head to bustling osterias where the jovial clatter and chatter offer an atmosphere that captivates all who enter. You'll learn it's vital to eat slow, savoring each bite as flavors melt and mingle on the palate.

To truly immerse in Tuscan gastronomy, dive into a hands-on experience such as a cooking class, where the secrets of homemade pasta, sauces, and traditional Tuscan desserts like cantucci (almond biscuits) are uncovered. Alternatively, explore a vibrant market. San Lorenzo Market or Mercato Centrale will introduce you to vibrant produce, freshly caught seafood from the Tyrrhenian Sea, aromatic herbs, and spices that define Tuscan cooking.

A venture into Tuscan cuisine is incomplete without sweet endings. Sample the delicate delight of panna cotta or the earthy, satisfying taste of chestnut-based cake. For a taste of something luxurious, indulge in panforte, a dense confection enriched with nuts and candied fruits, redolent of spices that dance on your tongue.

Whether riding through quaint villages or down bustling city avenues, the sights, smells, and tastes of Tuscan cuisine will beckon. Each stop unveils a new layer to this evocative culinary canvas, urging you to lean in farther, taste deeper, and let your gastronomic journey in Tuscany captivate every sense. Scooters offer the freedom to weave between these culinary invitations, each turning an opportunity to uncover a slice of this region's rich, flavorful narrative.

Local Markets and Street Food Adventures are at the heart of Tuscany's vibrant culinary landscape. They offer a sensory experience like no other, providing a real taste of local life. The bustling energy of a Tuscan market is infectious. Vendors proudly display their harvests under the morning sun while the smell of fresh bread wafts through the air. There's something inherently charming about the organized chaos: voices haggling over prices, the rustle of paper bags filled with treasures, and the laughter of children who run freely amongst the vibrant stalls. Each market tells its own story and reflects the unique character of its locale.

With scooters at your disposal, the world of Tuscan markets becomes your oyster. Scooters allow you to venture into the nooks and crannies of the region where the most enchanting markets often thrive. Imagine weaving through the narrow streets, catching glimpses of rolling hills and vineyards, as you head towards these local treasures. Every corner turned offers hints of what lies ahead—the earthy aroma of pecorino cheese or the rich scent of truffles in season. This isn't just about eating; it's about discovering and embracing the local culture through its food.

Every Tuscan town, no matter how small, is likely to have its own market day. In places like Florence's Mercato Centrale, you'll discover an overwhelming array of goods: freshly caught seafood, handmade pasta, and artisan cheeses. The displays are an art form, with colors so vivid they demand your attention. As you explore, remember to engage with the stall owners. They are eager to share their passion and stories behind their produce. They might even let you in on local secrets—like the best way to enjoy their olive oil or which tomatoes are just right for a panzanella salad.

Beyond the traditional markets, street food is an integral part of Tuscany's culinary fabric. It's where you'll find quick, delicious bites that pack a punch. There's a rustic authenticity to Tuscan street food that's hard to resist. Picture yourself stopping by a tiny cart in Siena to grab a rich and savory lampredotto sandwich, a Florentine delicacy made from tender tripe steeped in broth and perfectly spiced.

In coastal towns like Livorno, street food takes on a different dimension with seafood delights that honor the ocean's bounty.

Sample a bowl of cacciucco, a seafood stew that captures the essence of the Mediterranean. The robust flavors balance beautifully and leave a lasting impression. This is the joy of street food; it's convenient yet deeply rooted in tradition, extending an invitation to taste Tuscany's regional diversity firsthand.

The adventure doesn't stop with market visits and quick bites; it extends to learning about the roots of these delicious offerings. Take time to explore the history and stories behind the iconic foods and you'll find a richer understanding of Tuscany itself. Passionate food historians and vendors are often ready to share tales that connect you to the people who cultivated these culinary customs over centuries. It's not just about feeding the body; it's a feast for the soul.

An essential market experience lies in one of Tuscany's most famed wine towns, Montepulciano. Here, the markets include artisan products like homemade pasta and cured meats that are perfect travel snacks. And there's a certain excitement in discovering how these market staples synchronize with local wines, making your gastronomic journey all the more memorable. Local vintners often attend these markets, inviting you to taste their latest harvests, delighting your palate with rich reds and buoyant whites.

Empowering your journey through these local markets are tips and tricks for maximizing the adventure. It's wise to carry a reusable bag and a small knife for spontaneous picnics after a fruitful morning of market exploration. Wear comfortable shoes and be prepared to wander the cobbled paths that lead to unexpected culinary gems. Engage with the locals, ask questions, and be brave enough to try something new; you'll be rewarded with unforgettable flavors and experiences that enhance your Tuscan tale.

The street food scene across Tuscany reflects the region's adaptability and creativity in embracing new trends while maintaining a connection to ancestral roots. In modern cities like Florence, food trucks offer an eclectic mix of traditional and contemporary bites, allowing you to indulge while taking in historical sites on a scooter ride. An adventure in itself is trying crostini di fegatini, toasted bread topped with a rich chicken liver pâté. This snack perfectly encapsulates the blend of simplicity and complexity that defines Tuscan cuisine.

This journey through local markets and street food adventures paints a picture of Tuscany beyond its famed art and landscapes. It's the vibrant heartbeat of day-to-day life here, waiting to surprise you with joy at every pick-up-and-go stall or beneath each market awning. With a scooter as your companion, traversing this culinary trail becomes not just travel but immersion. It encourages you to dive deeper, taste further, and truly live Tuscany.

As you embark on this itinerary, consider blending market visits with culinary tours or classes, which many Tuscan towns offer. You'll not only taste but also learn to create some of these masterpieces under the guidance of skilled chefs. Engage with fellow travelers in these settings and share stories and tastes that leave not just a temporary delight in your mouth but a lasting connection to the region and its people.

Finally, let the spirit of discovery motivate you. Each market visit and street food encounter offers a chance to uncover another layer of Tuscany's rich character. Embrace the spontaneity that comes with venturing down unknown paths—only then can you claim to truly be a traveler of the world. With these experiences tucked into your backpack of memories, Tuscany will be more than just a destination; it becomes part of your culinary journey.

Cooking Classes on the Go blend seamlessly into the winding paths of Tuscany, offering an immersive experience that combines culinary art with a sense of wanderlust. Picture yourself riding a scooter through the sun-drenched hills of the region, with a gentle breeze guiding you towards a rustic kitchen nestled amidst vineyards or olive groves. These hands-on classes aren't just about learning to cook; they're about experiencing the essence of Tuscan culture and its profound love for food.

With every dish you prepare, you're essentially taking a time machine back to the roots of Tuscan cuisine. The recipes taught in these classes are often handed down through generations, preserving the authenticity and simplicity that Tuscan food is celebrated for. Imagine pulling over at a countryside villa or a quaint farm, where a nonna—a grandmother with decades of culinary wisdom—welcomes you with open arms. Her stories, as rich and satisfying as the food, add an unparalleled depth to the cooking experience.

Travelers seeking more than conventional sightseeing will find these cooking classes a refreshing departure from the usual tourist path. They offer an opportunity not just to observe but to engage actively with the local community. You chop, you simmer, you taste, all while standing beside fellow food enthusiasts from around the globe. It's a joyfully messy, sometimes chaotic process, but that's what makes it memorable. The laughter and camaraderie add flavor just as much as the fresh basil or ripe tomatoes.

One of the remarkable aspects of "Cooking Classes on the Go" is their mobility. No two classes are alike, just as no two Tuscan vistas are. One day you might find yourself surrounded by rows of grapevines, learning the secrets of traditional pasta. The next, you could be near the coast, concocting a seafood risotto with ingredients sourced directly from local fishermen. This dynamic approach keeps your itinerary flexible, allowing you to integrate cooking lessons seamlessly into your travel plans without being tied to a single location.

For the scooter enthusiast, these culinary stops can serve as delightful pit stops along your journey. They're not just centered around meals; they encompass the whole gastronomic experience—right from selecting the freshest ingredients at a local market to savoring the dish that's been deftly crafted. This hands-on involvement turns what might have been another meal into a flavorful chapter of your Tuscan adventure.

The vibrant landscapes of Tuscany provide an inspiring backdrop as you learn and cook. Each class celebrates the seasonal bounty of the region, emphasizing fresh, organic produce that reflects the Tuscan philosophy of food. Whether it's the late summer's harvest of sun-ripened tomatoes or autumn's bounty of wild mushrooms and chestnuts, these classes are a tribute to the land's generous flavors.

Participating in these classes also indirectly supports local farmers and artisans. Many classes source their ingredients locally, encouraging sustainable practices that benefit the regional economy. It's a cycle of giving and taking, where everyone, including you, contributes to safeguarding Tuscany's traditions while savoring its culinary delights.

Furthermore, these classes offer an intimate window into the nuanced cooking techniques that make Tuscan cuisine unique. Techniques such as balancing flavors, layering textures, and the art of slow cooking are best learned hands-on. Skilled chefs and locals will guide you through each step, sharing their passion and skill in ways that culinary books and videos can hardly replicate.

As your journey unfolds, these cooking classes could spark a newfound appreciation for Tuscan food, inspiring future travels and culinary experiments back home. Returning travelers often recount how the skills learned in Tuscany continue to influence their home cooking, turning ordinary meals into delightful reminders of their time in Italy.

From olive oil tasting sessions in the Chianti region to learning the intricacies of truffle hunting, the possibilities are as varied as Tuscany's landscape itself. Imagine folding butter-soaked dough with precision to prepare a flaky pastry, or mastering the art of crafting perfect ravioli under the guidance of a passionate chef who shares local traditions like a cherished narrative. Each class not only leaves you with new skills but also stories and memories you'll cherish long after the last bite.

In conclusion, "Cooking Classes on the Go" beckon you to dive into a culinary journey that awakens all senses. They're an invitation to move beyond the role of observer and become an active participant in a culture where food is a proud expression of identity and heritage. So, rev up your scooter, trail through the picturesque roads of Tuscany, and let these unique classes add a distinct flavor to your Italian escapade. Whether you leave with a new recipe or a profound sense of fulfillment, the experience promises to enrich your understanding of Tuscany's culinary soul.

For anyone yearning to combine their love for travel with a palate-pleasing adventure, these classes promise an experience that transcends mere sightseeing. It reminds us that the true essence of a place often reveals itself through its food, and the stories told around the table are ones that linger long after the journey ends.

So, gear up, wander into the heart of Tuscany, and let the spirit of adventure guide you from one culinary revelation to the next. It's a journey of flavors, stories, and the joyful pursuit of a meal prepared with love.

Chapter 7:
Art and Soul of Tuscany

As the sun dips below the rolling hills, casting a golden hue over ancient landscapes, Tuscany reveals its true masterpiece: a vibrant fusion of art and soul. This region, a muse for countless artists across centuries, offers more than just a visual feast. It's an emotive journey through time, where every fresco and stone echo stories of passion and creativity. Picture cruising on a scooter past grand basilicas and intimate chapels, with the whispers of the Renaissance trailing in the breeze. The allure of Tuscany's artistic heritage beckons not just from its grand museums but also from hidden artisan workshops sprinkled through picturesque villages, each one a canvas of everlasting inspiration. Whether you're exploring age-old galleries or stumbling upon a creative workshop, Tuscany immerses you in a living art gallery, urging you to seize every moment of beauty and expression on this unforgettable adventure.

Exploring Tuscany's Artistic Heritage is akin to diving into a living canvas where every brushstroke has a story. Tuscany is a bastion of artistic brilliance, a testament to human creativity that reflects centuries of history, culture, and unyielding passion. As you journey through this region on two wheels, the fusion of art and architecture enriches every mile, inviting travelers to not just view but feel the stories etched into the landscape.

Florence, the crown jewel of the Renaissance, doesn't merely house art—it breathes it. With your scooter parked nearby, take a leisurely stroll through the Uffizi Gallery, which houses masterpieces by Botticelli, Michelangelo, and Leonardo da Vinci. Yet, Florence's magic goes beyond the famous artworks. In the less frequented alleys, street artists add contemporary flair with vividly painted murals and installations, showcasing the city's evolving artistic narrative.

Continuing your journey, Siena calls out with its stunning Gothic architecture and medieval charm. The city itself is an artwork, with the Piazza del Campo at its heart—a unique shell-shaped square that plays host to the vibrant Palio horse race twice a year. The colors and symbols displayed in the contrade flags epitomize the artistic spirit embedded in Siena's cultural identity.

Venture further into the hills and discover that art thrives not just in grand galleries, but in local workshops and artisan studios. Small towns like San Gimignano and Volterra offer a different pace, where ancient towers reach for the sky, and alabaster craftsmen carve beauty out of nature's bounty. Watching a master potter or a skilled leatherworker can be a source of inspiration, as their hands deftly create pieces that blend traditional techniques with innovative designs.

Artistic heritage is also experienced through the landscape itself. The Tuscan countryside, with its rolling hills and cypress-lined roads, resembles a pastoral painting come to life. This natural splendor has long captivated artists, inspiring works from the pastoral depictions of the Renaissance to the impressionist interpretations of more recent times. As you ride through these landscapes, there's a sense of entering a world where nature and art coalesce seamlessly.

Don't miss the chance to explore lesser-known villages where art hides in plain sight within frescoed churches and quiet piazzas. Take, for instance, Pienza, considered the "ideal city" of the Renaissance, with its layout designed to reflect the harmony and balance sought after during that era. Here, art isn't confined to galleries; it's woven into the very fabric of daily life and the town's architectural ethos.

Beyond the visual arts, Tuscany's artistic heritage includes its rich contributions to literature and music. Cities like Lucca, the birthplace of composer Giacomo Puccini, echo with the strains of operatic genius. Meanwhile, cobblestone streets provide stages for lyrical storytelling and street performances, where tales of love, war, and life beckon audiences to pause and listen.

The Renaissance sparked a quest for knowledge, leading to an age where humanistic ideals were depicted through art in a way that still captivates us today. Nowhere is this more evident than in Tuscany, a vast classroom of the arts, inviting travelers to learn and reflect as they navigate its roads. Engaging with this artistic heritage offers a chance to connect deeply with humanity's past while contemplating its relevance in today's fast-paced world.

Finally, art in Tuscany is an invitation to participate. Whether you're kneading dough in a culinary class, capturing vistas on canvas through a plein air painting session, or partaking in a photography workshop amidst the olive groves, every creative endeavor enhances your connection to the region. It's this participation that turns a journey into an immersive experience, where you become both spectator and creator, adding your own chapter to Tuscany's ongoing artistic story.

Ultimately, "Exploring Tuscany's Artistic Heritage" whets the appetite for what's more to come—where each turn of the road reveals another layer of beauty and inspiration. Whether you're on a dedicated quest to see the very best of Tuscan art or happen upon it by chance, the region promises an artistic journey that is as rich and varied as the landscapes you'll explore. So embrace this adventure, let art guide your path, and allow Tuscany to leave its indelible mark on your soul.

Finding Inspiration: Artisan Workshops and Galleries in the heart of Tuscany is like unlocking a treasure trove of creativity and craftsmanship. As you zip through sun-dappled hills and picturesque villages on your scooter, each turn might lead you to an atelier where the smell of fresh paint mingles with the earthy scent of clay. Tuscany's tradition of artistry isn't just housed in its grand museums but lives vibrantly in these modest workshops scattered across the region.

Dive into the experience by visiting the artisan hubs of Florence, Siena, or San Gimignano. In these towns, winding alleyways open up to galleries that burst with color and innovation. Whether you find yourself captivated by the intricate mosaics, hand-blown glass, or the simple elegance of a meticulously woven tapestry, each piece tells a story of generations. These artisans often follow techniques that have been passed down over centuries, adapting them with contemporary flair. It's not just about seeing art; it's about understanding the heart and soul poured into every stroke and stitch.

Your Tuscan journey through art doesn't end with observation. Get your hands dirty and fuel your creativity by participating in workshops that invite you to try your hand at crafting your own masterpiece. Imagine molding a piece of the earth into a ceramic vase, or guiding molten glass into a shimmering sculpture—both a challenging yet rewarding testament to your time in Tuscany. These interactive sessions break down barriers, channeling your inner artist in ways you never expected.

In the quaint town of Lucca, known for its Renaissance walls and cobbled streets, you might stumble upon a local pottery studio. Here, artisans eagerly share their passion, introducing you to the delicate balance required to master the wheel. As you feel the clay glide beneath your fingers, you appreciate the calming rhythm that connects you to the traditions of old-world Europe.

The diversity among artisan studios is astounding. The craftsmanship varies from town to town, offering a portfolio as diverse as the Tuscan landscape itself. For those with an eye for fashion, the leathercraft schools in Florence will appeal. Rooted in a history of prestigious guilds, these studios continue to produce quality work that exudes elegance and durability. Perhaps you'll decide to make a bespoke piece yourself, marrying functionality with artistry in every stitch.

In the lush landscapes of the Chianti region, the passion for art and wine intertwines seamlessly. Some galleries here are more avant-garde, showcasing modern interpretations amidst the rustic viticulture. You'll find contemporary artists who draw inspiration from their vibrant surroundings, capturing the undulating hills and vineyards in abstract forms that inspire visitors to see Tuscany through a new lens.

Exploring these galleries and workshops gives you a glimpse into the heart of Tuscan life. Art is a reflection of culture and a testament to the endurance of tradition. As you ride your scooter from one town to the next, the landscape itself seems to be an artist at work, painting the sky in hues of gold and lavender at day's end. This blend of inspiration, history, and innovation is what makes Tuscany an unparalleled destination for those who appreciate the intricate dance between past and present.

Beyond the visual arts, music and theater performances are woven into the fabric of Tuscany's culture. In the town of Montepulciano, for example, intimate opera houses and outdoor venues provide a stage where classical music and contemporary pieces harmonize in perfect symphony. Here, the melodies echo the region's charismatic spirit and the creative pulse that beats strongly across its hills and valleys.

For the experimental and avant-garde, Tuscany offers spaces that push the boundaries of traditional art forms. The region hosts a vibrant community of interdisciplinary artists setting up shop in converted farmhouses and underutilized industrial spaces. These artist collectives offer shows that challenge and inspire, ensuring you depart with newfound perspectives and a richer appreciation of the artistic adventurous spirit.

Tuscan Sunsets: A Scooter Journey Through Italy's Heartland

Can't-miss locations include Florence's Oltrarno district, known for its artistic innovation and craftsmanship. Step away from the cathedral crowds to find boutique studios and galleries that thrive outside the mainstream. Here, artists work metals, sculpt forms, and paint daring works that fearlessly critique and question, igniting conversations long after you've left their thresholds.

These galleries and workshops become more than mere detours on your Tuscan exploration. They are places of profound connection and discovery, bringing you into the fold of a timeless tradition with practices that remain as alive and dynamic as the region itself. The time spent within them becomes personal, bridging the distance between spectator and creator, between itinerant and artisan.

The journey through Tuscany's artistic landscape is a reminder that while destinations and itineraries offer structure, the real magic often lies in the places discovered when you allow yourself the freedom to explore undeterred. As you throttle through winding roads, Tuscany's tapestry of artisan workshops and galleries reveals itself like hidden gems, just waiting to inspire the traveler willing to seek them out.

Chapter 8:
Festivals and Seasonal Events

In the heart of Tuscany, each season unveils a tapestry of festivals and events that invite exploration beyond the usual tourist path, offering an authentic taste of local life. Spring blossoms with the colorful *Scoppio del Carro* in Florence, where ancient traditions merge with modern-day celebrations. Summer heats up with the vibrant Palio di Siena, thrilling spectators as riders on horseback rush through the city's winding streets. Autumn uncorks the rich flavors of the grape harvest with festivities such as the *Chianti Classico Expo*, a wine lover's paradise. The chill of winter carries with it the warmth of the Mercato di Natale in Pisa, where local artisans share their crafts and culinary delights. Traveling by scooter adds a sense of freedom and adventure, allowing you to weave through towns and villages, uncovering hidden gems and joining spontaneous celebrations. Embrace the rhythm of the seasons, and let Tuscany's festivals fill your journey with stories and souvenirs that last a lifetime.

Calendar of Tuscan Festivities Tuscany is a land where time-honored traditions and vibrant celebrations intersect with the scenic beauty of the rolling hills and historic cities. Throughout the year, the Tuscan calendar is peppered with an array of festivals that warmly invite visitors to partake in local culture with open arms and ardent hearts. The people of Tuscany eagerly celebrate life's splendid moments through a blend of religious celebrations, food and wine fairs, and historical re-enactments. Whether you're zipping from town to town or setting up camp in one particular village, the region offers a bounty of events that promise unforgettable experiences.

Spring in Tuscany unfurls with a burst of color and festivity. One of the pivotal events is the 'Scoppio del Carro' in Florence, celebrating Easter with an explosion of fireworks shot from a cart—a spectacle deeply rooted in tradition that brings throngs of locals and tourists together in joyous celebration. As the rhythms of spring breathe new life into the countryside, villages like Certaldo welcome the 'Sagra della Cipolla', a delightful festival celebrating the sweet red onion with an abundance of culinary treats.

Summer, warm and lustrous, is synonymous with a bountiful harvest of festivals across Tuscany. The 'Palio di Siena' stands as one of the most renowned and thrilling horse races in the world. With Sienna's historic square as its stage, the Palio is more than a race; it's a captivating manifestation of medieval pageantry and fierce community spirit. As the sun reaches its zenith, Montepulciano hosts the 'Bravio delle Botti'. Here, competitors race through the steep streets pushing wine barrels—a spirited event that perfectly embodies Tuscany's love affair with wine.

Autumn drapes Tuscany in a golden robe, signaling the start of wine and olive oil festivals that draw enthusiasts eager to indulge in the fruits of the land. As grapes are harvested, the 'Festa dell'Uva' in Impruneta invites revelers to a grape-focused event filled with parades and tastings. Meanwhile, the camaraderie of olive oil enthusiasts ripens during these months, celebrated in events like the 'Festivals of the Olive' held in various locales like Lucca and Greve in Chianti. With every tasting, every dance, and every heartfelt interaction, you're woven into the rich tapestry of Tuscan culture.

Winter in Tuscany may be quieter, but it's no less magical. As December approaches, the countryside and cities alike glow with festive lights and the spirit of 'Natale'. The cities' piazzas are transformed into festive markets, where artisans display handcrafted goods, offering the perfect opportunity to grab a unique memento of your Tuscan adventure. Christmas is celebrated with joyous fervor, while smaller towns like San Miniato hold truffle fairs that highlight the white truffle, one of Tuscany's prized culinary delights.

Tuscany's reverence for its past and traditions is not confined to large cities alone. The quaint charm of village festivals such as the 'Medieval Festival of Monteriggioni' transport visitors back in time with medieval games, dances, and feasts. It's a vivid immersion into a bygone era, where modern life pauses to allow history to take the center stage.

Each of these festivals stands out for its individuality yet threads together a narrative of community, celebration, and shared history. Navigating Tuscany on a scooter provides you not only with an efficient mode of transportation but an immersive way to connect with these vibrant events. On two wheels, you can weave through the architectural beauty of Siena, Florence, and beyond, reaching the tucked-away gems where local festivals beckon with the promise of discoveries best savored up close.

Engaging with Tuscan festivities enriches your journey beyond mere sightseeing—it's a vibrant tapestry of encounters and experiences. Embrace the friendly atmosphere, try your hand at local customs, and maybe even join a parade. There's no better way to understand a culture than to live it, even if only for a moment.

In essence, the festival calendar of Tuscany is a living embodiment of its culture—an interactive gallery of music, art, tradition, and culinary delight. These events don't merely happen; they come alive, inviting you to savor their spirit. Let the exuberance of Tuscan festivities animate your travel stories as you set off on your own adventure, scooter beneath you, and the wind whispering tales of celebration in your ears.

Participating in Local Traditions in Tuscany is like stepping into a vibrant tapestry of history and culture, each thread woven with stories that echo through generations. Picture yourself riding a scooter through sun-kissed fields, the wind tousling your hair as you venture toward a celebration rooted in the ancient rhythms of the land.

Tuscany is renowned not just for its serene landscapes but also for its rich traditional events, where locals and visitors alike come together in joyous harmony. Participating in these local traditions offers a genuine taste of Tuscan life, a journey into the heart of its communities. You'll find yourself swept up in the passionate festivities and authentic rituals that reveal the region's cherished customs. From lively parades filling the cobblestoned streets with color, to tranquil gatherings honoring the land's bounty, each event is a window into Tuscany's soul.

Throughout the year, a calendar teeming with festivals beckons you to join in. It spans from the jubilant Carnival extravaganzas in Viareggio to the sacred Palio horse race in Siena. The Palio, in particular, is an electrifying spectacle, a tradition that dates back centuries. Held in Siena's iconic Piazza del Campo, it's not just a race but an expression of fierce civic pride. As the drums roll and flags flutter, the entire city pulses with anticipation, drawing you into its whirl of excitement.

Visiting Tuscany during its myriad seasonal events offers an immersive experience. You're not just a bystander but an active participant in living history. Engaging in these activities can evoke a sense of connection to both past and present. Take, for instance, the renowned grape harvest festivals, which unfold in various villages across the region every autumn. These celebrations commemorate the end of harvest season, inviting you to partake in age-old stomping rituals, taste fresh wines, and feast on local delicacies. It's a festive moment to relish in the fruits of the earth and community labor.

Beyond the major spectacles, there's a host of smaller, intimate gatherings that exemplify the essence of Tuscan traditions. For instance, in spring, the Maggiolata festival in Montepulciano showcases a beloved custom that celebrates the awakening of nature. Villagers dress in vibrant costumes, singing joyous songs as they parade through the flower-adorned streets. Joining in, you become part of a collective celebration of life and renewal.

Many travelers choose to align their journeys with these festivals, ensuring unforgettable encounters. Whether you're witnessing the pyrotechnic marvel of Luminara di San Ranieri in Pisa or the moving Infiorata in Pitigliano, where flower petals create breathtaking carpets of art and faith, these events magnify the allure of Tuscan exploration. They're a call to experience the enchantment of shared joy and artistry.

Participating in local traditions also allows for deep cultural learning. Each festival is steeped in symbolism and history, presenting opportunities to converse with locals and gain insight into their worldviews and way of life. Sharing stories and customs, you'll find warmth and hospitality at every corner, a welcoming embrace into the community.

There's also a delightfully pragmatic side to these festivities. They can act as hubs for local artisans, where craftsmen and women display their talents and wares. Amidst the celebrations, you'll discover intricate ceramics, handwoven textiles, and an array of culinary wonders. It's a chance to support local economies and take home unique mementos that carry the spirit of Tuscany with them.

For scooter enthusiasts, the journey to these events is part of the adventure. Navigating through picturesque routes with rolling hills and vineyards stretching into the horizon, each ride becomes a prelude to the vibrant experiences awaiting you. The flexibility a scooter affords means you can easily hop between different towns and villages, relishing the spontaneous discoveries along the way.

Tuscan Sunsets: A Scooter Journey Through Italy's Heartland

This remarkable opportunity to engage with local traditions enriches your travels in Tuscany immeasurably. As you dance amidst the crowd during lively music nights or relish the aroma of street food transforming lively squares, you're crafting your narrative within this enduring story of Tuscan life. These experiences leave a lasting imprint, reminding you that travel is not just about seeing new places, but about living and sharing in their essence.

In essence, each festival and tradition is a chapter in Tuscany's grand book of life, inviting you to turn the page. Whether you're painting your days with Tuscan colors at the festivals or savoring its rich tastes, you're contributing to and creating memories that echo long after you've left. It's this participation in the vibrant tapestry of Tuscan traditions that truly transforms a trip into a timeless journey. Your experience becomes as unique as a fingerprint upon Tuscany's enduring cultural canvas.

Chapter 9:
Natural Wonders and Outdoor Activities

Immerse yourself in the breathtaking natural splendor of Tuscany, where rolling landscapes and untouched terrain offer a playground for the adventurous spirit. The region's nature reserves and parks boast an array of vivid colors and serene vistas that beckon exploration on two wheels. Whether you're gliding past vibrant fields of wildflowers or pausing to admire the intricate patterns of olive groves, every turn reveals a new masterpiece painted by nature. Outdoor enthusiasts can diversify their journey with a mix of hiking, biking, or even a tranquil paddle on one of the many serene lakes. Each activity invites you to pause and breathe in the fresh Tuscan air, enhancing the invigorating sense of adventure. With every path explored, the unique marriage of natural beauty and the thrill of discovery transforms your journey into a tapestry of unforgettable experiences. All these wonders compel travelers to forge new paths while savoring the freedom that comes with every twist and turn, leaving you inspired long after your scooter ride has ended.

Tuscan Nature Reserves and Parks are places where you can breathe in the majesty of nature while rolling through a landscape that seems like it's been painted by the divine. Here, time slows down, allowing you to savor each moment, each sight, and each sound. Tuscany isn't just an artist's haven or a gastronome's paradise—it's a sanctuary of natural beauty.

Tuscan Sunsets: A Scooter Journey Through Italy's Heartland

Prepare to be awed by the *Parco della Maremma*, a natural masterpiece known for its coastal dunes, marshes, and rich wildlife. This reserve, located along the Tyrrhenian Sea, offers a delightful escape from the bustling historical towns. As you glide along on your scooter, the scent of Mediterranean scrub and the salty tang of the sea breeze fills the air. Perfect for those looking to plan a day of exploration and pure, natural delight, the park provides numerous trails of varying difficulty, catering to hikers with all levels of experience.

For a different kind of adventure, visit the *Casentino Forests, Monte Falterona, and Campigna National Park*. Situated in the Apennine Mountains, this expansive area offers dense forests and impressive views from its peaks. It's not just the physical landscape that's enchanting; there's an almost spiritual feeling that permeates the air here, steeped in history and mythology. With ancient hermitages and monasteries dotting the park, the sense of walking through time is palpable. The vast forest, mainly composed of beech woods, provides a serene backdrop for both quiet reflection and thrilling experiences.

Meanwhile, the *Val d'Orcia*, recognized as a UNESCO World Heritage site, captivates with its iconic rolling hills, cypress trees, and idyllic farmhouses. It's the picture-perfect Tuscany that lingers in your mind long after you've returned home. Navigating this region on your scooter allows you to truly appreciate the subtleties of its landscape—the way golden light filters through clouds or how ancient roads lead to tiny, welcoming towns. This area isn't just a place to see; it's a scene to feel deeply and remember fondly.

Tuscany is also home to the *Orecchiella Natural Park*, a haven of biodiversity set against the mighty Appennine peaks. Here, animals like deer, moufflons, and even the elusive golden eagle roam freely. With well-marked trails, it's a paradise for light trekkers and nature photographers keen to capture the perfect shot of sunrise over the mountains. Those interested in geology will be thrilled with the park's natural formations, including caves and unique rock outcrops.

For those eager to merge culture with nature, the *Arcipelago Toscano National Park*, which encompasses seven idyllic islands in the Mediterranean, is a must. Each isle offers its own blend of lush landscapes, crystal-clear waters, and fascinating history. Whether you're snorkeling amidst vibrant marine life or savoring locally caught seafood at a small seaside trattoria, you'll find that these islands embody a slower, more authentic way of life.

Another notable mention is the *Farfalle Nature Reserve* in the province of Prato. Known as "The Butterflies," this reserve is aptly named for the incredible diversity of butterfly species fluttering about. A walk or gentle ride through this reserve is like stepping into a living dream where nature literally dances around you. It's an unmatched opportunity to witness Tuscany's commitment to preserving its biodiversity.

These reserves and parks are not just about visual splendor—they offer a sensory symphony that leaves an indelible mark on your memory. Whether it's the rustling sound of leaves in a silent forest, the sight of deer springing gracefully through trees, or the captivating fragrance of sun-warmed wildflowers, Tuscany's natural spaces invite you to pause and absorb every detail.

Your adventure through these enchanting parks can take many forms. You could start your day at sunrise, venturing out on quiet trails as the world awakens, only to spend the afternoon unwinding by a tranquil lake. If you're a serious thrill-seeker, consider planning a full day of biking through rugged paths that test your endurance and feed your spirit. Each park offers an array of possibilities to cater to every preference and timetable.

Tuscan Sunsets: A Scooter Journey Through Italy's Heartland

Exploring Tuscany's reserves and parks on a scooter adds a dimension of pure joy and freedom to your journey. The moment you kick off and the breeze hits your face, you'll feel an exhilaration uniquely tied to this mode of travel. Scootering allows you to cover more ground than on foot and yet maintains the intimacy of a personal journey that a car simply cannot provide. You can stop at any of the region's scenic overlooks, hop off, and snap a photo or just soak it all in without the constraints of traffic or parking concerns. This is the ultimate way to engage with Tuscany's unspoiled beauty.

In addition, these natural spaces offer more than just scenic beauty; they hold stories and gifts that local guides and fellow explorers generously share. It's not uncommon to encounter tales of ancient Etruscans or legends of spirits that remain in the whispers of the wind through the trees. Engaging with locals or knowledgeable rangers can heighten your experience and connect you more deeply with the land.

Ultimately, navigating Tuscany's breathtaking nature reserves and parks offers everything needed to renew the soul. It challenges the adventurer in you, rewards the nature lover, and satiates the curious explorer. On a scooter, you are not just traversing a destination; you are intertwining with its essence, becoming a part of its living tapestry. So get ready to embrace Tuscany in its most authentic and unfiltered form as you ride through these heart-enveloping expanses. Revel in the moment, and let the Tuscan sun be your guide.

Hiking, Biking, and More offers adventure seekers a cornucopia of outdoor experiences amidst Tuscany's stunning landscapes. Imagine weaving through sunlit trails on a brisk hike or feeling the wind against your face as you bike along the undulating hills. This section encourages exploration of Tuscany's rural and natural areas, serving as a guide to the region's hidden outdoor treasures beyond what can be discovered from a scooter.

Well-Being Publishing

Start your journey in the heart of Tuscany, where scenic biking routes meander through emerald vineyards and silver olive groves. The area around Chianti is a great place for cyclists of all skill levels, offering both tranquil paths for leisurely rides and challenging routes for the more adventurous. The meticulously maintained trails are often lined with rustic stone walls and postcard-worthy views of rolling vineyards, punctuated by the occasional medieval hamlet.

For those who prefer to experience Tuscany on foot, hiking trails abound in its varied landscapes. The Garfagnana region, nestled between the Apuan Alps and the Apennines, presents a tapestry of landscapes, with trails that lead wanderers through ancient forests, over stark mountain peaks, and past serene mountain villages. Here, hikers can stumble upon wildlife such as deer and wild boar, and find themselves enveloped by nature's quiet symphony.

Another must-visit for hiking enthusiasts is the Val d'Orcia, a UNESCO World Heritage Site. Its paths drag you into dreamy fields strewn with poppies and iconic cypress trees. This picturesque valley offers both gentle walks and more demanding hikes, each providing an opportunity to reconnect with nature and appreciate the region's unspoiled beauty. Along the way, the ruins of medieval castles and the quietude of abandoned farmhouses provide a glimpse into the area's rich history.

For an adventure that combines history with breathtaking vistas, the Via Francigena, an ancient pilgrimage route, is an excellent choice. Stretching from Canterbury to Rome, the Tuscan section runs through enchanting landscapes, taking hikers through historic villages like San Miniato and the fortress town of Monteriggioni. Walking this trail is like stepping back in time, a journey marked by centuries-old chapels and relics from an era where pilgrims once tread.

While Tuscany's trails offer plenty for walkers and cyclists, they're just as accommodating to adrenaline seekers. For those craving more excitement, rock climbing in the Alpi Apuane will test your mettle and reward you with stunning vistas from high above. Tackle the limestone cliffs that challenge even experienced climbers, or take a guided ascent to learn the ropes in a unique setting.

In the warmer months, Tuscany's lakes and rivers open up a whole new world of adventure. Kayaking through the serene waters of Lago di Bilancino provides a tranquil escape, while more adventurous spirits might enjoy white-water rafting in the rapids of the Lima River. These aquatic activities offer a refreshing contrast to the heat, allowing both relaxation and thrill in equal measure.

Not to be overlooked, horseback riding offers a unique way to explore Tuscany's terrain beyond paved roads. Ride through open fields, cross gentle streams, and traipse through wooded hills, all while enjoying an intimate view of the environment. Several riding schools and stables offer lessons and guided rides for beginners and experienced riders alike, ensuring a memorable experience regardless of skill level.

For a truly unique exploration of Tuscany's outdoors, consider venturing underground. The region's karst landscapes are laced with stunning caves and grottoes, particularly the spectacular Grotta del Vento. Here you can discover the awe-inspiring world of stalactites and stalagmites, subterranean streams, and cavernous halls that stretch deep into the earth.

Taking the time to explore these natural wonders and outdoor activities not only enriches your travel experience but also deepens your connection to Tuscany's varied landscapes. Whether pedaling through vineyard-laden hills or hiking past centuries-old ruins, these adventures invite you to immerse yourself fully in the region. It's in these moments, alone or shared, that Tuscany leaves its most lasting impression, inspiring memories that linger long after your journey ends.

Well-Being Publishing

In the spirit of independent exploration, embrace the freedom and spontaneity that Tuscany's great outdoors offers. Pack a picnic, set out to discover a hidden trail, or simply breathe in the fresh, crisp air that marks a break from busy cityscapes. When venturing into the wild, the opportunities are endless, each path more inviting than the last, urging exploration and beckoning the curious traveler to step beyond the familiar.

Chapter 10: Accommodations and Authentic Stays

Exploring Tuscany by scooter offers travelers a unique opportunity to immerse themselves in the rich tapestry of this stunning region, and finding the right place to stay can transform the journey into an unforgettable experience. Whether you're winding through the sun-dappled hills or coasting along tree-lined lanes, accommodations abound that reflect the true spirit of Tuscany. From charming farmhouses that offer a glimpse into rustic Tuscan life to boutique hotels with sweeping vistas of olive groves and vineyards, every lodging choice becomes a story. Many travelers find that staying at an agriturismo, a working farm turned guesthouse, bridges the gap between comfort and authenticity, offering homemade meals straight from the farm and a taste of the slow life. Imagine waking up to the scent of cypress trees and sipping local wine as the sun sets over rolling landscapes. And for those drawn to the call of the wild, there are camping options where you can sleep under a blanket of stars, letting the gentle breezes lull you to sleep. Each type of accommodation provides not just a place to rest your head, but a doorway into Tuscany's unique cultural heartbeat, making your scooter adventure not just a trip, but a journey of discovery and connection.

From Farmhouses to Boutique Hotels is your guide to experiencing the authentic charm of Tuscany's varied accommodations. Picture yourself waking up in a farmhouse nestled among olive groves, or checking into a boutique hotel hidden in the winding streets of a medieval town. Each offers a unique lens through which you can explore this enchanting region, making your Tuscan adventure every bit as memorable as its captivating landscapes and rich history. Whether you're a cultural explorer looking to soak up local traditions or an adventure seeker in search of new experiences, these distinctive stays offer something for everyone.

Tuscany's farmhouses, or "agriturismi," provide an unparalleled entry into rural life. Many have been transformed into comfortable lodgings, where the charm of centuries-old architecture meets modern comfort. Staying at a farmhouse means more than just having a place to rest your head. It offers a chance to immerse yourself in the region's agrarian traditions. Wake up to the sight of farmers tending to fields and olive groves, then enjoy a breakfast of fresh, organic produce, often sourced from the land you're on. The sense of peace and connection to the land is palpable, and the intimate atmosphere invites you to slow down and savor each moment.

Your farmhouse hosts may even invite you to partake in some of the daily activities, offering a authentic experience of farmhouse life. Depending on the season, you might learn how to press olives into oil or join a wine harvest. Such experiences aren't just about doing something different; they're about connecting with Tuscany in a way that's both personal and profound. This is the perfect setting for those who wish to escape the hustle of urban living and find tranquility in simplicity. Plus, nothing beats relaxing with a glass of Chianti in hand, watching the sun set over the rolling hills.

If the rustic life isn't entirely your style, Tuscany's boutique hotels offer refined elegance and curated aesthetics in historical settings. These accommodations, often housed in carefully restored buildings, embody the spirit of the Renaissance with their artistic design and heritage appeal. You'll find them nestled in the heart of Tuscan towns like Florence and Siena, where history whispers in the walls and culture thrives in abundance. Each hotel is a story waiting to unfold, filled with character and thoughtful touches that promise comfort as well as style.

Staying in a boutique hotel offers its own kind of adventure. Histories blend seamlessly with contemporary culture, creating spaces that inspire and indulge. Enjoy breakfast in a courtyard kissed by the morning sun, or unwind in a suite adorned with original frescoes. These accommodations excel in offering personalized service, ensuring your stay is precisely tailored to your preferences. For independent travelers, this attention to detail makes every day special, allowing you to create the perfect balance between exploration and relaxation.

But no matter where you stay, the Tuscan ethos of hospitality runs deep. The locals pride themselves on providing travelers with an experience that's both welcoming and enriching. This makes every accommodation as much about the people you meet as the place itself. Conversations drift naturally over a shared meal or a casual chat, offering insights into local customs and stories of the land. It's a warmth that leaves a lasting impression, turning strangers into friends and enhancing your connection to Tuscany.

And did we mention the views? Whether commanding vistas of undulating vineyards from a hillside farmhouse or street-level perspectives from your city hotel, the scenery is breathtaking everywhere you look. Every town and countryside inch has its own allure, easily explored on a scooter, as you glide through scenic routes and pause at leisure to drink in the setting. This flexibility is one of the joys of scooter travel, giving you the chance to effortlessly shift from urban cafe culture to the rustic charm of the rural hinterlands.

As you travel from village to vineyard, from cobbled street to cypress-lined avenue, the diversity of Tuscany's accommodations becomes a travel narrative in itself. Each new stay offers a chapter of discovery and surprises. Embracing this patchwork of experiences encourages a journey that's fluid and adaptable – the very essence of independent exploration. In this process, you'll find that the places you sleep serve not only as resting spots but as integral parts of your adventure.

Ultimately, choosing where to stay while exploring Tuscany is about selecting how you wish to interact with this remarkable region. Each option, be it a historic farmhouse or a chic boutique hotel, offers an avenue of engagement that's as unique as Tuscany itself. The flexibility to craft your own path, coupled with the distinct accommodations available, means your adventure is whatever you choose to make it. So pack your bags, ready your scooter, and open your heart to the splendor that awaits; Tuscany, in all its varietal hues and hospitable warmth, is waiting for you to explore it fully.

Camping Under the Tuscan Sun offers a truly immersive experience for those seeking an intimate connection with Tuscany's enchanting landscape. Imagine waking up to the gentle rustle of olive branches, with the golden sun casting its first light over rolling hills, and the soft chirping of birds to welcome the new day. When you're camping here, every moment feels like a page from a storybook where adventure and serenity harmonize effortlessly.

Tuscany is famed for its stunning villas and farmhouses, but camping brings you closer to nature's heart. With the region's temperate Mediterranean climate, camping is not just feasible—it's delightful. The dry summers and mild winters mean you can be out and about at almost any time of the year. From rugged mountaintops to serene lakesides, there's a camping spot to match every preference. Grab your tent, pack some essentials, and set your sights on an authentic Tuscan adventure.

One of the most popular spots for camping is the Parco Naturale della Maremma, where wild boar and deer roam freely, and the coastline offers a refreshing breeze. Nestled on Tuscany's southwestern coast, the park provides a tapestry of diverse landscapes, from thick pine forests to sandy beaches. Whether you're pitching a tent under the shadow of the mighty Monte Amiata or setting up camp near the pristine waters of Lago di Burano, you'll find the perfect backdrop for a memorable camping experience.

What truly sets camping in Tuscany apart is the opportunity to engage with its rich biodiversity. The region is a sanctuary for nature lovers and adventure seekers alike. Imagine exploring hidden trails that weave through dense woods or cycling along winding paths that reveal panoramic vistas. As you navigate this picturesque terrain, you'll discover an ecosystem brimming with life. From the gentle flutter of the rare butterfly to the rustle of a squirrel darting up a tree, every moment spent outdoors is a testament to nature's wonders.

Nights under the Tuscan sky are just as magical. As the sun dips below the horizon, the landscape transforms into a canvas of soft hues. The stars begin their nightly dance, and the moon illuminates the rolling hills in silvery light. Campfires crackle softly, and the air fills with the comforting aroma of roasted chestnuts or freshly prepared pici—a thick, hand-rolled pasta that's a local favorite. It's the perfect setting for sharing stories, partaking in hearty communal meals, or simply savouring the tranquil silence that only nature can provide.

While camping in Tuscany, it's also worthwhile to explore nearby towns and villages. Quaint settlements like San Gimignano and Volterra offer glimpses into Tuscany's storied past. The narrow, cobbled streets and medieval architecture invite exploration, while local markets tempt with their vibrant produce and handmade crafts. Each day is a balance of adventure and relaxation, with the freedom to chart your course as you see fit.

For those looking to combine camping with a bit of luxury, consider "glamping" options available at several spots in Tuscany. Imagine sleeping in a well-furnished yurt or a charming cabin equipped with all modern amenities, yet still surrounded by nature's raw beauty. Such experiences marry the thrill of outdoor life with the comforts you might crave after a long day of exploration. These unique accommodations often come with additional perks like farm-to-table meals, guided nature hikes, or even yoga classes held amidst olive groves.

Safety, of course, is paramount when camping. Before venturing into the Tuscan wilderness, it's wise to plan ahead. Ensure your tent and gear are suitable for the terrain and climate. Familiarize yourself with local wildlife—especially around areas where boar and deer roam—and respect their habitats. It's advisable to carry a good map or navigational tool, as well as an ample supply of water and sun protection, particularly in the peak summer months.

Camping in Tuscany isn't just about spectacular landscapes and warm sunny days. It's an opportunity to disconnect from the digital world and embrace a slower pace of life. It's about the simplicity of cooking dinner over an open flame and the camaraderie found around a campfire. Most importantly, it's about creating moments—whether it's catching a sunrise over the vineyards, or laughing with newfound friends under a starlit sky—that will linger in your memory long after the trip ends.

Whether you're an experienced camper or a novice setting out on your first adventure, Tuscany promises an experience that will inspire and rejuvenate. It's a journey into the heart of one of Italy's most beloved regions, where history, culture, and nature intertwine to craft an unforgettable tapestry of exploration and relaxation. So let the Tuscan sun be your guide, and set off on an adventure that promises not just to enrich your travels, but perhaps to also transform your perspective.

Chapter 11:
Extended Routes and Day Trips

Exploring Tuscany on a scooter opens up a world beyond the well-trodden paths, giving adventurers the ability to carve their own journey through the region's heart. With the freedom of two wheels, you can escape to breathtaking locales often overlooked by guidebooks. Imagine riding through the enchanting Val d'Orcia with its sweeping landscapes or venturing to the majestic Apuan Alps, where rugged trails meet serene vistas. These routes invite you to dive into Tuscany's lesser-known corners and experience the raw beauty and authentic culture that lies beyond crowded spots. This way, each day trip becomes a canvas for unique discoveries—from intimate villages rich with history to expansive fields where time seems to slow down. By planning meticulously and injecting a dash of spontaneity into your itinerary, your scooter adventure in Tuscany transforms into a personal odyssey, filling each moment with wonder and inspiration. Whether you're seeking peaceful solitude or vibrant local interactions, these extended routes offer the perfect escape, allowing every twist in the road to tell its own story.

Planning Your Tuscan Itinerary sets the stage for crafting an adventure that seamlessly melds spontaneity with a well-thought-out game plan. When you hit the open road on a scooter, the world unfurls at a pace that's perfect for absorbing the essence of Tuscany's splendor. Start with a broad brush of what you want to see and do, then refine your vision into an itinerary that feels both purposeful and flexible. Bask in the freedom that two wheels afford and let them guide you through a terrain filled with diverse landscapes, from the whispering hills of Chianti to the bustling artistic quarters of Florence.

First, consider what drives your curiosity. Is it the art and architecture, the serene countryside, the culinary delights, or perhaps a combination of these? By determining your main interests, you can focus your energy on the most fulfilling experiences. Tuscany's rich tapestry means you may find yourself splitting your days between cultural excursions and moments of sheer relaxation. For instance, spend a morning exploring Siena's medieval streets and an afternoon tasting wine in Chianti's sun-dappled vineyards. Each day becomes an episodic adventure, woven together by the roads you choose.

Next, identify the core areas you want to explore, and think of them as the building blocks of your journey. Florence and Siena often form the backbone of Tuscan itineraries, offering abundant art, history, and local flavor. However, don't be afraid to stray from traditional paths to uncover smaller towns and hidden gems. Consider including towns like San Gimignano, with its famous towers and lush surroundings, or Lucca, with its Renaissance walls perfect for a scenic ride. These lesser-known spots often hold the surprise elements that enrich your travel narrative.

Flexibility is key while planning—set goals but allow room for the unexpected. Perhaps you'll stumble upon a charming cafe that draws you in for an impromptu tasting, or you might extend your stay in a town simply because it feels right. Keep a day or two unplanned as a buffer for new discoveries or just to rest and soak in your surroundings. This balance between structure and spontaneity ensures that your journey through Tuscany is both richly rewarding and personalized.

Charting your itinerary also means being practical about distances and travel time. Tuscany's rolling landscapes are picturesque but may take longer to traverse than expected, especially when traveling by scooter. Allow sufficient time for each leg of your journey, including short breaks to linger over views or just a breather from driving. Map out your stops not just by destination but by the route and roads—some offer breathtaking vistas that you wouldn't want to miss.

The changing seasons in Tuscany further influence what should be included in your itinerary. Spring and autumn are particularly magical, with milder temperatures and blooming vistas. Meanwhile, summer invites you to bask in the region's sunny embrace, ideal for beach excursions and alfresco dining. Don't overlook the winter months; they lend a cozy charm as towns are less crowded, and you can savor more intimate experiences at various markets and events.

Incorporate thematic days into your itinerary to delve deeper into specific interests. A day centered on Tuscany's artistic heritage could include visits to Florence's renowned galleries like the Uffizi, while another might be dedicated to the gastronomic wonders of the region, perhaps visiting a local market followed by a hands-on cooking class. Each day serves to enrich your understanding and appreciation of Tuscany's multifaceted culture.

Explore the possibility of connecting with locals who can offer insights or guided tours that align with your themes of interest. Engaging with residents provides enriching narratives and perspectives that can't be found in guidebooks. Whether it's a vineyard owner sharing the story of their land or an artisan explaining centuries-old techniques, these encounters transform a journey into a tapestry of stories.

Finally, leverage technology to enhance or simplify your planning process. There are myriad apps and platforms to help map routes, find accommodations, and discover points of interest. Even with a meticulously planned itinerary, keep an element of flexibility; after all, travel's true spirit often lies in the unforeseen turns. Remember that each ride is a story yet written, awaiting your discovery. Embrace it with all the senses alive to Tuscan breezes and sights.

Must-See Destinations Beyond the Beaten Path invite those craving adventure to venture off the well-trodden routes and explore the Tuscany you won't find in every travel guide. This section celebrates the charm of lesser-known locales and even more secluded spots that offer unique perspectives of the region. Whether you're gliding over sun-dappled hills or winding through ancient forests, each destination promises an unforgettable experience.

Picture yourself on a leisurely ride to Val d'Orcia, a UNESCO World Heritage site known for its stunning landscape of rolling hills and cypress avenues. While many flock to tasting rooms in Montalcino, a scooterist's heart belongs to the unpaved roads connecting isolated abbeys and whispering forests. Here, history melds effortlessly with nature, and each turn reveals a panorama just waiting to be captured.

Don't miss the hidden charms of Montefioralle, a medieval haven nestled in the Chianti hills. This tiny village, untouched by time, invites exploration on foot once you park your ride. The narrow cobblestone streets wind past ancient stone houses, leading you to vistas that make the journey worthwhile. Indulge in local delicacies at a small trattoria, savoring the flavors that seem to capture the essence of this peaceful enclave.

Head towards the Lunigiana region, a land of mystery and legends. Known for its castles and ancient villages, Lunigiana promises a trip through history. The roads here might not be the easiest, but the rewards are rich: discover the enchanted village of Fosdinovo with its imposing castle that looms over the landscape, ready to share stories of yore with those who listen intently.

Tuscan Sunsets: A Scooter Journey Through Italy's Heartland

For a breath of fresh air, consider the Pratomagno mountain range. As you ascend its slopes, the air grows crisp and the views more expansive, with vistas that stretch across the Arno Valley to the peaks of the Casentino. The scenic ride to the Croce del Pratomagno, a monumental iron cross, is a pilgrimage of peace and introspection. It's the kind of journey where the road itself becomes the destination.

Near the town of Saturnia, immerse yourself in the thermal hot springs nestled in the landscape like nature's own spa. Known for their healing properties, the cascading pools of warm water offer a rejuvenating retreat away from the bustling city scenes. Relax and soak under the sun, surrounded by the serenity of untouched Tuscan countryside.

Then, there's the coastal adventure along the Costa degli Etruschi. While the main beaches are well-known, it's the remote coves and hidden beaches accessible by scooter that stir the wanderlust. Discover secluded spots where the turquoise waters meet rocky shorelines, perfect for a tranquil seaside picnic or a private swim.

Another must-see is the town of Poppi, seated atop a hill in the Casentino Valley. With its exquisite medieval castle, Poppi offers a glimpse into Tuscany's feudal past. Surrounding it are extensive trails perfect for hiking or scooting through lush landscapes, punctuated by picturesque vineyards and olive groves.

The Garfagnana, lying to the northwest, boasts rugged landscapes and dense forests perfect for the adventurous soul. Move through the Apuan Alps, discovering quaint villages like Castelnuovo di Garfagnana. Encounters here feel like stepping back in time, with traditional lifestyles preserved in the culture and cuisine.

Tuscany's serene side unveils itself in the region around the Monte Amiata volcano. While relatively quiet compared to its famed counterparts, it offers panoramic views, historic chestnut forests, and trails that lead to hidden sanctuaries. Pause and listen to the whispers of ancient trees - they have countless tales to share.

A visit to the masked splendor of Barga, a colorful village tucked away in a remote corner of Tuscany, leaves an indelible mark. This vibrant cultural hub draws musicians, artists, and wanderers alike. Explore its winding streets and admire the breathtaking views of the Serchio Valley from its hilltop perch.

Embrace the call of mystery with a voyage to the village of San Gimignano, slightly off the main tourist grid. While its famed towers draw many, venture a bit further to the surrounding trails and vineyards to retreat into solitude and unspoiled beauty. Each ride through the blooming fields paints a scene reminiscent of Renaissance artwork.

In essence, Tuscany reveals its most delicate charms to the traveler willing to get lost. While the major attractions beckon, it's the minor roads and nameless paths that shape stories of adventure, creating bonds between the rider and the landscape. Venture beyond the beaten path and discover your personal slice of Tuscan heaven. The open road awaits, with promises of new surprises around every corner.

Chapter 12:
Tips and Tricks for the Savvy Scooterist

As you navigate the rolling landscapes of Tuscany, there are a few insider tips that can elevate your scooter adventure from memorable to downright unforgettable. Keep your scooter in top shape with routine checks—check tire pressure often, carry a basic toolkit, and know the contact of a local mechanic just in case. When faced with an emergency, having a backup plan will be your lifeline; make a digital copy of your documents, know the nearest hospitals, and have a translator app ready to bridge any language gap. Embrace spontaneity but plan for those scenic detours—often, the less-traveled paths offer up Tuscany's magic in ways guidebooks can't describe. Lastly, don't forget to contribute online reviews; your experiences could shape another traveler's dream journey. While you ride through sunlit vineyards or explore quaint historical towns, remember that these small yet significant acts prepare you for anything, letting your heart soak in the pure essence of Tuscany.

Maintaining Your Scooter on the Road is as much about foresight as it is about responding to the needs of your trusty two-wheeled companion as they arise. Whether you're winding through the Chianti hills or venturing through the storied lanes of Siena, keeping your scooter in top shape ensures that your journey through Tuscany remains carefree and captivating. Before setting off on your Tuscan journey, there are proactive steps you should take to minimize the need for roadside maintenance. Check your scooter's fluid levels, brakes, and tire pressure. A quick once-over can make a significant difference.

Trust me, you don't want to be caught off-guard when you should be soaking up sun-dappled vistas.

While traversing the Italian countryside, keeping an ear out for unusual noises is your first line of defense. Any irregular clinking, buzzing, or thumping might signal that something's gone awry. For instance, a persistent squeal often links to brake issues, whereas a rattling sound may be a loose accessory. If you encounter any of these auditory clues, it's best to pull over at a safe location and conduct a brief inspection. Carrying a basic tool kit with a few key essentials like a wrench, screwdrivers, and a tire gauge can make all the difference in these situations.

Imagine yourself winding through the sunlit paths of Tuscany when you feel a slight wobble in your handlebars. This is often an indication of tire stress or imbalance. Checking for punctures or unusual wear and tear can save your trip from becoming a nightmare. For those unfamiliar with fixing a tire, there's no shame in stopping by one of Tuscany's many small but proficient local repair shops. Not only might you get your scooter fixed, but you'll also experience the warmth of Tuscan hospitality firsthand.

On longer day trips, setting a schedule for routine stops not only offers a chance to stretch your legs and savor roadside attractions, but also to give your scooter a mini check-up. Re-evaluate tire pressure and fluid levels. Keep an eye on your fuel gauge. While a scooter's tank may be small, the thrill of exploring can make it easy to overlook this crucial detail. Planning your route with an awareness of fueling stations will mitigate the risk of an inconvenient halt in your adventure.

Tuscany's climate can be wonderfully varied, which can impact your scooter maintenance needs. In summer's peak, the heat may cause tires to expand, making regular pressure checks even more vital. In contrast, the cooler shoulder seasons of spring and autumn may incite condensation in your fuel tank. Using a fuel stabilizer can prevent moisture build-up and subsequent engine problems. Adapting your maintenance to the changing seasons is as vital as having the right protective gear for yourself on the road.

Electrical issues, though less common, can be equally vexing. Ensure your scooter's lights and signals work correctly, especially if you're exploring after dusk when Tuscany's winding roads are at their most tranquil. Carry spare bulbs and fuses, as power outages can happen at the most inopportune times. A quick bulb replacement can restore visibility and security in mere moments, allowing you to continue chasing those memorable Tuscan sunsets.

Brake maintenance is not to be underestimated. Being attuned to your scooter's ability to halt promptly can prevent mishaps on steep roads and winding descents. If braking feels sluggish, and adjusting the brake cables doesn't help, it might be time to replace the brake pads. Always prioritize safety to ensure that every journey on Tuscany's roads is a joyful and secure experience.

No maintenance guide would be complete without addressing the unforeseen—it's always wise to be prepared for emergencies. Know the emergency services number in the areas you're exploring, and carry essential contacts like local scooter repair services. Having a backup plan gives peace of mind and can transform a potential dilemma into a minor detour. The appendix of this book provides a valuable directory of services to keep at hand.

Lastly, cultivating a rapport with your rental provider can yield dividends. Many rental services in Tuscany offer quick workshops on essential scooter maintenance, ensuring travelers are the best prepared for their journeys. These sessions are genuinely invaluable, equipping you with insights tailored to your specific model and the areas you plan to visit. Plus, fostering a relationship with your rental shop means you'll have an immediate ally should unexpected issues arise on your journey.

In essence, keeping your scooter in top shape is about merging practicality with a dash of wanderlust. The richness of Tuscany awaits, with each road leading to new stories and untold adventures. Be it maintaining your ride or embracing spontaneous encounters, the heart of Tuscany beats in the seamless marriage of preparation and exploration. So, dive into your Tuscan journey with confidence, knowing you're ready for everything the road might present.

Dealing with Emergencies While the dream of scooting through Tuscany's sun-drenched landscapes can be idyllic, it's crucial to embrace the unpredictable nature of travel. You're here for an unforgettable adventure, and part of that involves being prepared for the unforeseen. Trust me, with a little preparation, you can navigate through minor mishaps and more serious situations with confidence, ensuring your journey continues smoothly. Let's explore practical steps and invaluable tips to keep your Tuscany adventure on track, no matter what life throws your way.

One of the first things you'll want to do when planning your trip is to familiarize yourself with basic first-aid procedures. Having a compact first-aid kit stowed in your scooter is a smart move. Stock it with essentials like band-aids, antiseptic wipes, insect repellent, and a small supply of over-the-counter pain relievers. It's a simple measure, often overlooked, but immensely valuable when you're miles away from the nearest pharmacy.

Beyond the first-aid kit, let's talk about scooter-specific tools. A portable repair kit can come in handy. Equip this kit with a tire pressure gauge, a multi-tool with various-sized Allen wrenches, a small flashlight, and if space allows, even a tire patch kit. Knowing how to use these tools is just as important as having them, so familiarize yourself with minor repairs before your journey.

An essential skill for any scooterist is knowing how to change a tire, and frankly, it's easier than it sounds. Start by practicing a quick tire change in the comfort of your lodging before venturing far. Scooters aren't heavy, and you might be surprised how simple it is to loosen a few bolts and swap a flat tire for a fresh one. Confidence in this basic mechanical skill will serve you well and minimize stressful roadside situations.

While mechanical issues can be problematic, getting lost in Tuscany's winding roads might initially seem more romantic than alarming. Still, it pays to be prepared. Modern navigation apps, pre-downloaded maps, and a good old-fashioned paper map should form the trifecta of your navigational toolkit. Each has its strengths—apps like Google Maps provide quick directions, pre-downloaded maps are lifesavers when your cell signal fails, and paper maps offer a broad perspective at a glance. Each has its role, and together, they lessen the chance of you staying lost for long.

Sometimes, though, technology can fail. In such moments, having a sense of your surroundings can be invaluable. Pay attention to landmarks in towns you traverse; the leaning tower of Pisa, the rolling hills of Chianti, or even a particularly memorable vineyard. These landmarks not only provide a cognitive map but also anchor your journey in Tuscany's rich tapestry.

Perhaps one of the more daunting scenarios is dealing with emergencies related to health. Should you experience or witness a more serious incident, having a list of local emergency contact numbers—such as the Italian emergency number 112—will expedite the process of getting the assistance you need. Familiarizing yourself with key phrases in Italian will also prove advantageous. Simple words like "aiuto" (help), "ospedale" (hospital), and "farmacia" (pharmacy) can be crucial in a pinch.

In case of a breakdown in more remote areas, a bit of resourcefulness goes a long way. This is Italy, a place celebrated for its hospitality. Don't hesitate to approach locals—they're often more than willing to help a wayward traveler. Just a friendly gesture and a smile can bridge the language barrier, and you might even find yourself with a newfound friend along the way.

Now, let's imagine that your scooter simply refuses to start, despite all the precautionary measures. Contact your scooter rental agency immediately. Most agencies in Tuscany are well-equipped to handle such emergencies, having a network of mechanics throughout the region. Keep your rental agreement handy as it usually contains emergency numbers and procedures to follow.

Aside from situational prep, maintaining your calm is vital. Stress can cloud judgment, especially in unfamiliar territory. Take a moment to breathe, assess the situation logically, and then take action. Break the incident into manageable steps—problem identification, possible solutions, and then execution. Remember, mishaps are just another story in your travel narrative.

Lastly, consider travel insurance that covers road emergencies and health incidents. It might feel like just another expense at first, but the peace of mind it provides is truly unmatched. Knowing that you have support if needed allows you to focus more on the exhilaration of the open road and the beauty that unfolds with every twist and turn of Tuscany's enchanting routes.

Embracing the unexpected is part of what makes adventure so thrilling. You've got the tools, the knowledge, and the resolve to handle emergencies with grace and efficiency. By preparing for any contingency, you free yourself to immerse fully in the Tuscan splendor, carving memories into the landscape of your journey that you'll cherish forever. Safe travels as you explore, knowing you're ready for anything on this great Tuscan escapade.

Online Review Request for This Book As you relish the freedom of your Tuscan scooter adventure, we invite you to share your

Tuscan Sunsets: A Scooter Journey Through Italy's Heartland

experiences and thoughts through an online review, helping fellow travelers find their own paths to unforgettable exploration.

Sunset Reflections and the Road Ahead

As you sit back and reflect on your journey through Tuscany, there's a certain magic that lingers in the air. The sun setting over the rolling hills casts a warm, golden hue on the landscape, offering a perfect backdrop to your thoughts. Traveling by scooter has been not just a mode of transport, but a companion that gave you the freedom to explore at your own pace. It's in these moments of serenity that the beauty of Tuscany crystallizes, promising to remain etched in your memory forever.

This journey brought together the rustic charm of the countryside and the vibrant pulse of centuries-old cities, creating a tapestry of experiences unique to this Italian gem. You felt the wind in your hair as you cruised through vineyards and olive groves, pausing to take it all in whenever a scene caught your eye. From immersing yourself in art in Florence to basking under the sun on the Etruscan Coast, each experience was a story unfolding on two wheels, yours to narrate as you wish.

In many ways, Tuscany taught you as much about yourself as it did about its territories. By embracing the unpredictable elements of scooter travel, you became more adaptable, more curious. And wasn't it wonderful to challenge the conventional in search of the extraordinary? You packed light, both literally and metaphorically, prioritizing memories over material things. Each town, each road, and each encounter enriched your understanding of this place, enhancing your appreciation for life's simple pleasures.

Tuscan Sunsets: A Scooter Journey Through Italy's Heartland

Consider how this journey may have changed you. Perhaps you've gained an appreciation for the slow rhythms of life, a stark contrast to the nonstop buzz of modern existence. You might find yourself inspired to carry this mindfulness into your daily routine, savoring each moment with the same delight you experienced while navigating Tuscany's landscapes. The diversity of experiences —from the bustling market stalls to the tranquil countryside —showed you the harmony of contrasts and the joy found in stepping beyond the ordinary.

The cultural wealth of Tuscany offered a deeper, more enriching view of life. Understanding and participating in local customs allowed you not just to see Tuscany, but to feel it. You learned that travel is not just about seeing new places but also about experiencing them and growing in the process. This adventure, with its many roads and paths, was as much a journey within as it was a geographic exploration.

Looking forward, consider how these adventures could extend beyond Tuscany. Every destination has its own tapestry of landscapes, culture, and history waiting to be explored, and a scooter might just be your key to gradual, immersive travel. Use the skills and insights gained on this journey to plan future adventures, whether in Italy or elsewhere. The world awaits, and with each trip, you unravel new stories, adding layers to the narrative of your life.

Indeed, there's no better teacher than the road itself. With each turn and twist, you've learned to appreciate the unpredictability of travel, finding comfort in spontaneity and joys in the unexpected. The scooter was your bridge between the known and the novel, a conduit to increased freedom and enriched experiences. Who knows what thrilling paths lie ahead, waiting to be discovered, open to the spirit of those willing to ride them?

It's not a goodbye to Tuscany, but a see you later. The timeless beauty of this land will always call out to you, inviting you back for more moments of discovery and joy. As you plan your return or adventure into new horizons, the lessons and memories from Tuscany will inspire every decision, every path chosen. They've become a part of you, as inseparable from your being as your love for exploration.

So here's to the sunset reflections, fueling dreams and weaving wanderlust into the essence of who you are. Here's to roads yet traveled, skies yet admired, and the endless possibilities that await. With Tuscany as your muse, let this journey be just the beginning, the opening chapter to a life crafted with adventurous spirit. Let these memories propel you towards new explorations, carried by the wind, driven by the heart, and vividly colored by the sunsets ahead.

Appendix A:
Appendix

As your Tuscan journey unfolds, this appendix is designed to be your steadfast companion, ensuring you make the most of every twist and turn in this enchanting region. Here, you'll find a curated collection of useful phrases and language tips that will help you navigate conversations with ease, adding a touch of local flair to your adventure. Whether you need to ask for directions or engage in spirited discussions over a robust Tuscan wine, these linguistic tools will have you ready to blend in. Additionally, we've compiled a list of emergency contacts and invaluable resources, offering peace of mind as you traverse the Tuscan terrain. And for those in need of a trusty steed, a detailed scooter rental directory awaits, featuring options that cater to every preference and budget. With these insights and tools at your fingertips, you'll be empowered to dive deep into Tuscany's wonders, ensuring each day is a page-turning chapter in your travel story.

Useful Phrases and Language Tips Exploring Tuscany on a scooter can be a truly rewarding adventure, especially when you've got a few handy Italian phrases up your sleeve. You'll find that Italians are generally warm and welcoming, but speaking even a little of their language can open doors that might otherwise stay closed. In this section, we'll dive into some useful expressions and language tips to help you navigate vibrant markets, charming towns, and lively festivals across the region.

First, let's start with some basic greetings. A warm "Ciao" is your go-to for a casual hello or goodbye, but if you prefer a more formal approach, "Buongiorno" (good morning) and "Buonasera" (good evening) are perfect alternatives. When it comes to saying thank you, "Grazie" is always appreciated, while "Per favore" keeps things polite when you're making a request. These polite gestures go a long way and help foster a positive interaction with the locals.

Ordering food and drinks is a major part of any Tuscan adventure. Imagine sitting in a cozy trattoria with the aroma of freshly baked bread filling the air. Knowing how to ask for a menu, "Il menu, per favore," or order a glass of wine, "Un bicchiere di vino, per favore," will enhance your culinary experiences. And of course, never leave without trying "gelato" – asking for a scoop of your favorite flavor with "Un gelato, per favore" turns a simple purchase into a delightful experience.

Getting around requires a bit of logistical language. If you find yourself in a charming village and need directions, asking "Dov'è..." meaning "Where is...," followed by your destination, usually inspires helpful directions. Similarly, at a scooter rental shop, communicating your needs clearly can make a difference. Try "Vorrei noleggiare uno scooter," meaning "I'd like to rent a scooter," to make your intentions crystal clear.

Let's not forget about safety. Knowing phrases such as "Ho bisogno di aiuto" (I need help) or "Chiamate un'ambulanza" (Call an ambulance) can be crucial in case of an emergency. It's always good to be prepared, even if the chances of needing these phrases are slim. And don't worry about pronunciation—most Italians appreciate the effort, and they're often willing to lend a hand even if your Italian isn't perfect.

Engaging with locals enhances your travel experience in Tuscany. Whether browsing a local market or attending a quaint town fair, expressions like "Quanti anni ha?" (How much does it cost?) and "È possibile provare?" (Is it possible to try?) come in handy. Interacting with vendors and artisans on a personal level often turns a simple purchase into an enriching story.

Additionally, cultural sensitivity in language can show respect and curiosity. When being introduced to a local tradition, using "Posso fare una foto?" (Can I take a photo?) honors both their culture and individual privacy. These small gestures of courtesy through language create a bridge between cultures, fostering understanding and friendship.

Lastly, practice makes perfect. Use any opportunity to practice your Italian, even if it's just small talk with a barista. This not only boosts your confidence but enriches your journey. Remember, language learning is an adventure of its own, with triumphs and mistakes alike contributing to the tapestry of your travels.

With these phrases in your repertoire, you're more than equipped to show respect and appreciation for the culture you're exploring. As you traverse the picturesque landscapes of Tuscany on your scooter, let these language tips guide you deeper into the heart of the region, transforming each encounter into a meaningful exchange. Embracing the local language elevates your journey from simply sightseeing to truly experiencing all that Tuscany has to offer.

Emergency Contacts and Resources As you set out to conquer the picturesque roads of Tuscany on a scooter, having a robust understanding of emergency contacts and resources is vital for a smooth and safe journey. Tuscany, with its rolling hills and enthralling towns, is an adventurer's paradise, but even the savviest traveler can encounter unforeseen hiccups along the way. From medical needs to mechanical support, knowing whom to call or where to go can turn a potential obstacle into a minor detour rather than a significant derailment.

If you find yourself needing medical assistance while exploring the Tuscan landscape, the emergency services can be reached by dialing 112. This is the universal emergency number within the European Union and connects you to local medical, police, or fire services. It's essential to communicate your location clearly, so having a good grasp of basic Italian phrases can be incredibly useful. Most operators speak English, but a little effort goes a long way in ensuring quick and efficient help.

For non-urgent medical issues, pharmacies in Italy, known as "farmacie," provide a wide range of over-the-counter medications and healthcare products. Farmacie are easy to spot by the green cross sign and their knowledgeable staff can assist with minor ailments and advice. In larger towns, 24-hour farmacie are available, promising peace of mind no matter the time of day. Keeping a list of the nearest 24-hour pharmacies in your travel itinerary ensures that help is always within reach when you're out indulging in Tuscan adventures.

Roadside assistance is another critical emergency resource to have at your fingertips. Tuscany's roads can be both enchanting and challenging, with their winding paths through isolated countryside. If your scooter experiences a breakdown, contacting a local roadside assistance provider is crucial. You can reach major service providers, such as ACI (Automobile Club d'Italia) by calling 803 116. Before heading out on your journey, ensuring your scooter rental includes roadside assistance or coverage is a wise decision that can prevent headaches later on.

In addition to professional services, local scooter rental businesses can be valuable resources in a pinch. They often have partnerships with local mechanics and can assist with minor repairs or troubleshooting. Many rental companies are accustomed to dealing with tourists and offer English-speaking support, which can ease the stress of handling mechanical issues in a foreign country. Establishing a rapport with your rental provider at the outset can pave the way for seamless support when needed.

For situations involving lost property or theft, be sure to contact the local police department, known as "Carabinieri," or the "Polizia." Filing a report can be a necessary step for insurance claims. Though Tuscany is generally safe, keeping an eye on your belongings and being aware of your surroundings, especially in crowded areas or tourist spots, is always prudent. Keeping a digital copy of your passport, travel insurance, and scooter rental agreement can assist with every process if physical documents are lost.

Beyond the immediate avenues of aid, it's beneficial to connect with the local expat or travel communities, both online and in-person. Platforms such as online forums, social media groups, and local meet-ups not only offer practical advice but also provide emotional support. Many travelers have traversed similar challenges and can offer insights that aren't found in guidebooks.

Lastly, don't underestimate the power of preparation. Before setting out each day, check weather forecasts and map out your intended route. This helps mitigate avoidable obstacles such as sudden weather changes or road closures. Having an updated and offline map application on your smartphone ensures that you won't get lost even in Tuscany's more secluded regions.

In summary, while Tuscany offers a spectacular backdrop for scooter adventures, preparing for emergencies allows you to focus fully on the breathtaking views, centuries-old olive groves, and the incredible art that dots the landscape. Navigating through potentially tricky situations with the right contacts and resources ensures your time in this extraordinary region is unforgettable for all the right reasons.

Well-Being Publishing

Scooter Rental Directory Nestled in the heart of Tuscany, an area known for its rolling hills and captivating landscapes, the scooter becomes not only a means of transport but also a companion in discovery. In this section, we lay the groundwork for a memorable exploration of Tuscany by presenting a carefully curated directory of scooter rental services. Whether you're in the bustling streets of Florence or the serene expanses of the Val d'Orcia, finding the perfect scooter to match your journey is essential. With a network that's as diverse as the artisans and winemakers scattered across the region, this directory serves as your trusted guide.

When embarking on a Tuscan adventure, it's crucial to know the rules of the road, but even more important is finding a reliable partner in your scooter rental. As you peruse this directory, consider the type of experience you wish to have. Are you drawn to the vintage charm of a Vespa, the symbol of Italian romance and freedom? Or perhaps a modern electric scooter, which effortlessly blends sustainability with practical mobility, fits your vision? Whatever your preference, this directory has been designed to cater to every explorer's needs, ensuring that the journey is as enjoyable as the destination.

Let's begin with Florence, a city renowned for its artistic legacy and renaissance flair. The buzzing streets house several reputable rental services, each offering a fleet of scooters to satisfy every taste and requirement. One standout service, Vespa Florence Rentals, offers classic scooters that evoke the nostalgia of La Dolce Vita, while ensuring modern-day reliability. Their customer service is often praised for its detailed instructions and safety recommendations, making it an excellent choice for first-time riders.

In Siena, a city that rivals Florence with its medieval charm, you'll find another gem: Siena Scooter Co., specializing in guided tours and solo rentals. Their fleet includes eco-friendly options, perfectly suited for navigating Siena's narrow, winding streets. Adventurous travelers might consider extending their hire to include the neighboring regions, given Siena's unique position as a gateway to southern Tuscany's treasures.

Further down south in the rolling fields of Chianti, explore Buon Viaggio Scooters, a family-owned establishment known for its warm hospitality and robust lineup of bikes. Whether you aim to wine-hop through the vineyards or meander through olive groves, their scooters promise to carry you with style and ease. Perhaps you've always dreamt of leisurely cruising along scenic routes, stopping spontaneously to capture panoramic views or sip on a perfectly brewed espresso in a local café.

On the coastal front, the Etruscan Coast boasts an array of rentals dedicated to those partial to seaside adventures. Coastal Cruisers Rentals provides a diverse selection, enabling explorers to traverse beaches, embark on island escapades, or simply ride along the stunning Tyrrhenian coastline. Their partnership with local eateries means you not only get transport but also insider tips on the best seafood pasta and gelato spots!

Of course, safety and logistics are paramount. With this in mind, most rental outlets offer an array of gear including helmets and protective wear, adhering to local safety regulations. Several also propose briefing sessions or companion apps offering real-time navigation support and tips for scooter novices. While some purists may disdain technology interference in a puristic Tuscan experience, others find it a valuable ally in safeguarding their journey.

Moreover, many rental businesses listed here go beyond providing a ride. They aim to enhance your Tuscan experience by offering personalized itineraries and recommending local events and attractions. It pays to enquire about packages that might include vineyard tours, culinary class partnerships, or tickets to theatre and art shows.

Beyond personal rentals, if you're planning a group adventure or a corporate getaway, several services offer specials on bulk hires, inclusive guided tours, and even catering for private events. Imagine a team-building exercise following the Chianti wine trail or a family reunion exploring hidden medieval towns. Special discounts frequently apply for extended rentals, also allowing for cost-efficient handling of longer-term visits.

In the quieter countryside of Montalcino or the rugged expanses of the Crete Senesi, smaller rental operations offer personalized experiences and authentic interactions with Tuscan locals. You'll often find an unrushed approach to customer service, with friendly proprietors eager to share stories of their Tuscan upbringing and local lore—a perfect chance to practice those useful Italian phrases from the earlier appendix section.

It's important to remember that the joy of scooting around Tuscany isn't solely about the mechanics, or even the destinations, but rather the serendipitous encounters each ride presents. Every winding road is an opportunity to stumble upon a quaint village festival, discover an artisan workshop, or simply enjoy a moment of quiet amidst nature's splendor.

One last note: while planning your scooter adventure, remain aware of the differing policies among rental services regarding licenses, insurance, and deposits—it's prudent to ask upfront to avoid surprises. This directory endeavors to assist in those initial stages, providing contact details and reviews where available, as a preface to hands-on research.

Ultimately, this section aims not only to connect you with rental options but to inspire confidence in crafting your very own Tuscan tale. As you set out on this two-wheeled journey through time and terrain, we hope it's the spirit of exploration and freedom that accompanies you at every turn and stop. Enjoy the ride!

www.ingramcontent.com/pod-product-compliance
Lightning Source LLC
Chambersburg PA
CBHW032046290426
44110CB00012B/971